I0073884

Change Is in Order

Change Is in Order

WHAT I LEARNED AS A LEADER IN A MALE-DOMINATED INDUSTRY

Karen Mooney

Copyright © 2017 by Karen Mooney

Karen Transforms
League City, Texas

ISBN: 0692820884
ISBN 13: 9780692820889
Library of Congress Control Number: 2016920829
Karen Transforms, League City, TX

All rights reserved. No part of this publication may be reproduced, stored in a retrieval system, or transmitted in any form, or by any means, electronic, mechanical, recorded, photocopied, or otherwise without the prior written permission of both the copyright owner and the publisher of this book, except by a reviewer who may quote brief passages in a review.

The scanning, uploading, and distribution of this book via the Internet or via any other means without the permission of the publisher is illegal and punishable by law. Please purchase only authorized electronic editions and do not participate in or encourage electronic piracy of copyrightable materials. Your support of the author's rights is appreciated.

Printed in the United States of America.

I dedicate this book to my husband, Keith, and to all the women colleagues I have the joy of learning alongside. All have greatly influenced me and my journey.

Contents

Acknowledgments

So much of the content of this book is a result of support from and interactions with many people. First and foremost, my husband, Keith, who continually encouraged me to pursue anything that serves my passion. As you can imagine, having a support system at home makes taking risks a whole lot easier. My high school basketball coach, Clyde Wallace, had a profound impact on me and set the tone for my leadership voice. I will be forever grateful that he came into my life. Lynne Watkins brought me out of my fog, and Laura Licato coached me to discover clarity of my calling. Paul Stanford was my first mentor and sponsor, and I am in his debt. Last, but not least, Eva Saenz and Lisa Tannehill showed me—through their bravery and courage—how to honor my voice.

Introduction

The goal of writing this book is to share what I have learned as a leader in the construction and facilities-management industries—both of which are still very much dominated by men. I graduated from college in 1992, so my experience spans the late nineties to the present day. It took me twenty years and many missteps before fully developing the leadership voice I have today, and I still learn something new every day. When I began my career, there were not a lot of female role models in the field, and I found myself feeling my way, trying to figure out the path. And while *now* there are so many resources and networks available to women in construction, engineering, facilities management, information technology, and oil and gas—all fields historically dominated by men— the concepts and lessons I learned are still applicable today. Many of the concepts presented here may not be new to you, but having them consolidated into a single source will help any woman hoping to learn to understand herself, to connect with a network, and to be a successful leader.

How to Read This Book
Because I process in small chunks, this book follows that same style. There are three parts. The first section is focused on you. To be a

leader in any industry, having awareness and understanding of who you are and what you stand for are fundamental cornerstones. The second section is all about community. Creating the impact you want relies on finding and building connections with those who share your passion and your support. This section provides resources and inspiration for you to take the next step in your leadership journey.

The final section provides different areas for you to reflect on as you define your own leadership voice. While this book is from my perspective as a woman leader in traditionally male industries, the principles apply to everyone.

Each chapter has a summary along with action steps, so you can skip around and use what is most useful to you. I've left room for you to add your own takeaways and action items from each chapter. Finally, my style is one of fun, humor, and silliness. While reading, if you find a passage that strikes you as a joke, trust me—it is. I wanted to write a book that was both informative and fun. Enjoy.

PART I

It's about You

You cannot transform yourself, and you certainly
cannot transform your partner or anybody else.
All you can do is create a space for transformation
to happen, for grace and love to enter.
—ECKHART TOLLE

I navigated the first half of my life thinking I knew myself. I knew
what I liked and what I didn't; I had a style and personality that were
clear. I had a great job, was happily married, and had the requisite
two dogs and a house. Then one day a personal event happened to me.
It threw me not only off my game but also down a well. It complicated
both my work life and home life—but more about that later. In a well, of
course, it's dark, and the path out isn't clear or easy. I was trapped by the
emotional turmoil and despair. All I wanted to do was get out. But when
you're thrown down, it's not always so easy to get back up.

Over the next three years, I worked hard to right my ship, which
had been tossed about by a hurricane. I quickly realized that no one
was feeling what I was feeling and that the only person who could fix
it was me. While it may have started out as a personal-development
project, it was soon incredibly obvious that I must first understand
myself before I could lead authentically. Hence, the reason I am going to start with the first step of knowing yourself: how to do it and
why it matters.

CHAPTER 1

Know Thyself

> There are three things extremely hard:
> steel, a diamond, and to know one's self.
> —Benjamin Franklin

E arly on, my husband and I lived in a "starter" home. Starter homes are usually small, older, and described by realtors as "quaint." They aren't. The kitchen had 1970s yellow linoleum flooring and yellow plastic laminate. And while it functioned well enough, it just wasn't our style. Luckily, we are both handy people and love projects. Before we knew it, the countertop was ripped out, the sink was on the driveway, and the coffee pot was in the bathroom. As we looked at the cabinets that remained, we realized the wood was not good quality, so out it went.

And once you have the cabinets demolished, you might as well deal with the flooring, right? At that point, we realized that we weren't sure our marriage was strong enough to handle a major renovation! During this time, we also realized some of the studs were in poor shape and needed to be replaced.

Yep, you guessed it. The project that had started as a simple update quickly mushroomed into an all-out renovation project. And as we recognized the investment we were about to make—in both money and personal effort—we knew we had to ensure that we were starting the rebuild on solid ground: going all the way down to the concrete floor and strong stud walls. After a long year of living with a torn-up kitchen, I'm happy to report the project turned out great and that—more importantly—our marriage survived.

Obviously, I don't recommend that you undertake a project as we did without knowing the boundaries first. But surprisingly, many of us approach our careers and personal lives by starting down a similarly disjointed path. We don't have clarity about our self-foundation, so we end up working at jobs, companies—or even living in towns—that aren't aligned with what we want. We start building without doing so on a solid foundation. Symbolically, we may replace the cabinet doors but never deal with the cabinet boxes; and while the cabinet doors still function, deep down, we know it is only a surface job. When you take the journey to become a leader of any kind—in business, as a parent, or even being the leader of your own life—it requires starting with yourself.

Many people have uttered the phrase, "I still don't know what I want to do when I grow up." Sometimes it's said with excitement and abandon as the person sees endless possibilities. More often than not, however, it's because the person feels incongruent in his or her life. The missing elements of fulfillment and clarity weigh on them and provide a sense of feeling lost. Before you can find your way in life, you must first spend time on yourself—a key step that is often sped through or—worse—skipped entirely.

This is the first chapter because it's the foundation of everything for you and about you. It sets your direction and provides the goalposts for your life—something very few spend time truly articulating. So, let's get started.

Are You Aligned with Your Values?

If I asked you right now what your values are, could you articulate them? Would you say the common ones, such as integrity and honesty or something silly, such as chocolate? Or would you first go to Values.com, look at all the words, and then decide which ones resonate with you?

To lead authentically, you must be acutely aware of all your values and seek to ensure alignment with them. It's when you have alignment with your values that you live with purpose. Unfortunately, I find that most people don't have true clarity of what values they want to honor. Most of us, when asked, will say that we share common values, such as kindness, compassion, and loyalty, but we are much more complex creatures than can be explained by simply picking from a stock list of values.

Where do values come from? They begin with your parents who instill in you character-building traits such as honesty and responsibility—and then an older sibling comes along and tries to undo it! Values may also come from your religion, culture, and the community (or multiple communities) in which you were raised. But someone just telling you what your values are doesn't make it so. As you mature, gain life experiences, and go on bad dates, your values are further refined and honed.

Here's an easy exercise to help you gain awareness of some of your values. Think of your favorite movie. It could be a drama, romantic comedy, or even a documentary. Which character most resonates with you in that movie? What is it about that character that you connect with? What do you admire about him or her? The answers are pointing to what you value. For example, I love the movie *Get Shorty*. I most connect with John Travolta's character, Chili Palmer. What I like about him is that he's funny, always thinking about possibilities, and he adapts to events on his way to achieving his goal of making his movie. From that, you can probably tell that I value humor, creativity, and adventure.

Take about fifteen minutes and journal yours. Just keep asking yourself, "What is it about Harry Potter that I connect with? And why is that?" Don't worry about anyone else's judgment about your answers—they don't matter. This is only about you and for you. It can be a silly character in a silly movie, or it can be a story of a survivor. What you are drawn to is the clue. My husband cannot turn off any show, movie, or documentary about World War II. He values being a part of something bigger than himself, so he is naturally drawn to celebrating his and others' military service. Stop now and do some writing to see what comes alive for you.

Another exercise you can do to identify values is to think of a peak moment in your life. It could be recent or from long ago. The moment should be a time when you felt most alive, in "the zone," totally energized, and at peace with who you were at that moment. For me, it was about two years ago, when I was teaching a class. I felt as though I had mastered the material; the students were laughing and connecting with the content and were totally engaged and ready to take action. I felt as if I was serving a bigger purpose for the organization and the industry.

From that experience, I realized additional values of inspiration, relationships, fun, growth, personal development, and a higher purpose. My articulated values are different from what parents normally instill in their children. They are a product of who I am and who I am meant to be. You can judge mine if you want; I really don't mind, because they are mine and not yours, and I wasn't seeking approval!

Now combine your lists from both exercises and work to get them present in your life. How do you feel when you read them? Do they resonate? Do you find yourself smiling as you read them or maybe feeling energized? How do you make your values more visible in your everyday life? Easy ways such as taping them to the mirror so you see them every morning, making them your screen saver on your computer monitor, or better yet, using them as a computer password. These are *your* guideposts, so make them visible. They are what matters to *you* and no one else. The unique combination is what brings *you* energy.

Another thing to remember: Your list is a living document and will change over time. Your list of values will become better honed as you become more aware of your values and where your energy is coming from. You may have started out simply with a value of "family" but then further clarified that to be "time with my family." The more you define your values, the more powerful they will be for you.

Where Are You Now?

As you develop your list of values, rate each on a scale from one to ten, with one being, "I am not honoring it as much as I want to," and ten being: "I am fully honoring it." I'll use an example. One of my values is fun. I feel full of life when I have fun. For me, fun is laughter, humor, playing games, or just being silly. It can be difficult, however, to work in some silliness with the business of life. I would give myself a four for fun. I get some fun in the day or week but not nearly as much as I want. Here is a simple worksheet example to get you started.

Worksheet Example

Rank in Order of Priority	Value / Need	Honoring Score Scale of 1 to 10 (10 = Highest)

Rate where you are now for each value, and then choose which one you want to increase. You may want to take a four to a six or an eight to a ten. Just choose whichever one you want to see some movement in (and don't feel obligated to pick the lowest number; choose the one that resonates with you). Once you have the new target, set a one-week goal to do activities that increase the honoring of your value. Maybe your value is inner peace, and your one-week goal is to meditate each day for ten minutes.

Now shift to your job and career. Are they aligned with your values? If you value relationships, but you spend eight hours a day doing data entry alone in a cubicle, you cannot lead authentically. If you value peace and quiet, you may not enjoy leading a large team of salesmen and saleswomen. These are extreme examples, but believe me, every day there are people going to jobs that drain the life from their veins for the simple reason that there is not alignment between their values and the work they are doing.

Connecting with the Values of Your Company

As I mentioned, we develop our values early on in our lives from a number of influences, and often, the biggest ones are our parents. Two of our values—integrity and caring—at my current learning laboratory are parenting 101: meaning parents generally instill in their children the values of honesty and being nice to others. When employees join the company, it's very easy to connect to those two values, as there is a high probability that new employees' values align with our own values. Our character outside working hours aligns with the character expected of us during the workday.

However, the third value—discovery—is different for some. For those in the profession of science or medicine, discovery may already overlap with their value systems, so alignment is welcomed. For the rest of us, there may not be an overlap, and thus, the gap must be recognized and resolved. What if you're the type of person who finds grounding and solace in consistency?

You may not enjoy the activity of discovery or be as comfortable exploring the unknown with abandonment. The phrase that follows *discovery* in our printed literature is: "We embrace creativity and seek new knowledge." Again, it's about where creativity and seeking new knowledge fall within your personal value system. For someone who loves to learn, seeking new knowledge and discovery may come naturally. And if you're blessed with having endless ideas, then perhaps you can't even turn off your creativity! But for others, both principles may be a little more outside their comfort zones.

Let's say you're working on a team to fix an issue. How comfortable are you with embracing new knowledge if you have concerns about the person providing that knowledge? Can you separate the two? Applying creativity to problem solving can be threatening to some as it usually results in change, and change is usually only embraced when the present state is no longer tolerable. My challenge for you is to consider how the values of your organization align with your own values. Is the match high or low?

There isn't a right answer; it's just additional awareness about the degree of alignment. If they don't overlap with your personal values, do you need to make a change in companies, and if not, how will you reconcile it? This is important to acknowledge, and yet so many do not. They may enjoy the work, but there is no passion and no loyalty to the company and its mission. Spend some time reflecting on your company's values. And if you own your own company, can you articulate what your company stands for? Do you hire staff with alignment of values in mind?

What Are Your Talents and Strengths?

This seems easy enough; just take a personality assessment, right? If you haven't done one of these yet, sooner or later, someone from human resources shows up and offers one to the team. They are intended to show you who you are, how you lead, how you learn, and how you handle situations. A few examples include: the Myers-Briggs Type Indicator, the Management Team Role Indicator, the Leadership Effectiveness & Adaptability Description, the Thomas-Kilmann Instrument, and the DISC personality test.

Needless to say, there are countless assessments we can take to tell us who we are. It seems the only thing missing is submitting a DNA swab to find out our ancestry. With all these assessments, it seems impossible to remember "what" you are. They each use different acronyms for their results so you have to remember whether you are you an ISTJ, an S2, or just an R2D2. It all can be just too much.

There is one more to add to the mix that is different from the others you know. It's different because it's easier to remember, easier to understand, and easier to apply. It's the Gallup StrengthsFinder assessment, which identifies your natural talents. The assessment is powerful because it also gives you the tools to understand the talents and strengths of others, allowing us as leaders to better understand work situations and ensure that the right people are in the room to solve the challenges we face daily. Some talents naturally collide—for example, context and futuristic—but knowing that before the team is assembled makes it easier to anticipate issues.

StrengthsFinder is a tool created by Gallup, Inc. based on the findings of the late Donald O. Clifton who is known as the "father of strengths-based psychology." The goal is to support people and groups in understanding and applying individual and collective talents to improve their relationships, increase their creativity, productivity, and overall happiness. It was first launched by Clifton and Marcus Buckingham in their book, *Now, Discover Your Strengths*, in 2001.

But a key clarification is in order: the terms *strengths* and *talents* are not interchangeable. A strength is the ability to consistently provide near-perfect performance in a specific activity, which you actually like to do. Talents are naturally recurring patterns of emotions, thoughts, or actions that can be productively applied. When you take a naturally occurring talent and add knowledge and skills—along with the time spent practicing (i.e., investment), developing your skills, and building your knowledge base—this transforms a talent into a strength.

Gallup identified thirty-four talent themes utilizing common terms so they are easy to understand and remember. They are: achiever, activator, adaptability, analytical, arranger, belief, command, communication, competition, connectedness, consistency, context, deliberative, developer, discipline, empathy, futuristic, harmony, ideation, includer, individualization, input, intellection, focus, learner, maximizer, positivity, relator, responsibility, restorative, self-assurance, significance, strategic, and WOO (an acronym for "winning others over").

What is so powerful about knowing your talents is that you can quickly assess which activities give you energy and which drain you. Do you prefer to work alone or alongside others? Do not make the mistake of asking your parents, friends, or local bartender, "What would you say are my talents?" Take out the subjectivity and get the objective answers.

There are multiple books to provide you a wealth of additional information as well as Gallup's podcasts that dive deep into each talent theme. Head over to GallupStrengthCenter.com and purchase an assessment for less than twenty dollars. It'll be the best money you've spent on yourself since that tattoo. If you are interested in learning more about talents and strengths, purchase most any Gallup book on strengths, and you'll get a free code to take the assessment.

The assessment will identify your top five talents, and for additional money you can unlock the rest of your thirty-four. But it's not necessary; the top five will provide enough information to guide you.

Once you know your own talents and which other talents can often collide with yours, the fun begins. What if your project team includes someone who must plan things in advance and you're the one who starts without even thinking about having a plan—how do you keep your sanity? Even if you don't know your talents, you know who you like and don't like working with, right? The key is understanding that it's not about you—I know, *shocker*!

The other person is not trying to make your life miserable; he or she is working the way that comes most naturally to him or her. Keeping that in mind, it becomes easier to shift focus to the end goal and have each contribute in the way that works best for him or her. This is not easy and not for the impatient. But developing this skill is what will take you from a contributor or manager to a leader. So, next time someone approaches something differently than the way you would, tell yourself that this is your leadership moment. Focus on the end goal and provide the space where each can contribute in the way that comes most naturally to him or her.

There are no right or wrong talents. Just because a talent is not in your top five, it doesn't mean you don't have it. It just means it doesn't come as naturally for you. It will be harder, take more time, and zap your energy for you to complete that particular task. It doesn't mean you can't balance the checkbook; it just means that some love to do it and others avoid it until the bank calls. You know who you are.

But you may be asking yourself, "Why do I need to do that? I already know what I'm good at." Do you really? Have you relied on others, such as a supervisor, to tell you? What if you have a talent that has never been nurtured or suppressed? What if your talent is "command," but as a young girl you were called bossy? Do you think it was developed? Of course not. Your talents are a source of energy. When you spend more of your day working from the talents that come naturally to you, you enjoy the day more and are less stressed, which will result in a healthier and happier well-being. Who doesn't want that?

Often, it's most fun to learn by a story. Let me give you a personal example that illustrates application of the concept of talents.

Living with an Activator

My sweet, dear husband of over twenty years, Keith, has the talent "activator" in his top five talents. Gallup describes Activator as "impatient for action," and "willing to start without knowing all the information or details," because they know they must get started to make things happen. Activator is not as high on my talent profile; it is more toward the middle, but often my top talents combined with his activator talent make life fun in the Mooney house.

In an effort to continue to improve my health, I bought an exercise bike for my home gym. Keith rips the box open (not opening it by the seams, mind you; he just rips the top and down the edges in any random way, so right off the bat, my organization gene is hyperventilating), and he lay all the parts out on the floor. Since it was my bike, I had the task of putting it together. Keith sat in the chair and provided commentary.

So as someone who is organized (that's the talent of "discipline"—which I have in my top ten), I first get out the instruction manual, of course, and begin to follow the instructions as they are presented. Mr. Backseat Driver over there says things like, "I'd put the seat on first." But that's not what the instructions said to do first. Then he said, "See, that piece fits into that piece over there and slides into the slot." Meanwhile, I'm trying to keep my focus (and sanity) and follow the instructions!

You have to know, Keith has a brilliant, mechanical mind; he can just look at things and figure out how they go together. He can grab the right size wrench by just looking at the bolt; he doesn't need to read the edge of it. When he takes things apart, he doesn't put the bolts in order so he can find them later; he throws them in a box, and then when it's time to put things back together, he looks in the box, and nine times out of ten, he grabs the right screw or bolt and proceeds to assemble. As you might guess—this *drives me nuts*! (Pun intended.)

You must remember, though, that talents allow us to work in the way that makes *us*—not the other person—most comfortable. He's comfortable just winging it so he can get started; I'm comfortable laying out a plan first. Now we haven't had to have couples therapy—yet—but we have found a comfortable place where these two talents, which are often at odds, can coexist. Keep in mind that we are married, so the law says we have to coexist!

Give or Sieve?

Because talents come naturally for us, they are sources of energy, and it's important that your activities align with your talents as much as possible. The more time you spend working from your talents, the less stressed you will feel, and the more you will accomplish in less time.

There is an easy exercise you can do to see where you fall on the continuum. Take a piece of paper and draw a line down the middle. At the top left, write *give*, and on the right, write *sieve*. Keep the sheet at your desk, and as you go about your day, capture activities that you are enjoying and that are giving you energy under *give*. Conversely, list those tasks that drain your energy like a sieve. Monitor yourself for a week or so, and see what new revelations you have.

I had a coaching client who did this exercise. She quickly realized that as a "people person," she gets energized being around and talking to people. What she decided to do was ensure that at the beginning and end of each day, she would do something that would connect to her colleagues. In some cases, it was simply catching up while she was getting her coffee or making a phone call to a customer. Now, she starts and ends her day energized and feeling great. She implemented a simple thing that has changed the way she feels each day.

You are a complex person. There is no single answer to who you are and what matters to you. I like to use the analogy of taking a road trip. You are a car heading down the road; your vehicle represents you at your best—operating from your talents and full of energy and power. Along the edges of the road are your values. They are what keep you in the center and ensure that you don't drive off into a ditch. And as we travel the road of life, just as when we're driving, we often can't see around the corner or anticipate when a fog will descend and impede our visibility. Clarity and alignment to our values and talents keep us not only centered on the road, but also our life. It is that personal navigation system that provides us our life fulfillment and is the basis to lead authentically.

Key Takeaways

- You must build your leadership style on a solid foundation, which begins with knowing yourself thoroughly.
- Spend time to fully identify your personal values.
- Seek alignment with your values: are your actions in your life honoring your values? Alignment with your values honors your authenticity.
- You will have more fulfillment in your life if the company you work for—or the company you lead—aligns with your personal values.
- Know your talents and actively work to turn them into strengths by adding knowledge and practice.
- People operate in the way that is most comfortable to them (and not solely to annoy you). Knowing yourself thoroughly will make it easier to work with those different than you because you will be able to identify the difference in talents.
- Learn which activities give you energy and which act as sieves and drain you.
- People who spend more time working in their talents are less stressed, have more energy, and experience more fulfillment.

My Takeaways

_____

_____

_____

_____

_____

_____

_____

_____

_____

Action Steps

- Identify your values either through the exercises provided or self-awareness.
- Make your values list visible in your life. Post them where you will see them every day.
- Identify how much you are currently honoring your values. Choose one you want to increase and identify what you will do to honor it more fully.
- Determine if your company's values align with your own. Do you need to make a change? Do you need to reconcile the difference?
- Take the assessment at GallupStrengthsCenter.com to find your top five talents. Read the material provided and understand how your talents are working for you and when they hold you back.
- Do the give/sieve exercise for a week. What did you learn or confirm about yourself?

My Action Items

_____

_____

_____

_____

_____

_____

_____

_____

_____

_____

_____

_____

CHAPTER 2

Self-Care Is Not Selfish

Caring for myself is not self-indulgence; it is self-preservation, and that is an act of political warfare.
—AUDRE LORDE

I have always been drawn to the concept of meditation. Something about seeing statues of a meditating Buddha while shopping would cause me to walk by and usually check the price. Growing up, I didn't know anything about meditation or even yoga. That was just not a topic that made it into the conversation in South Texas in the seventies But as I grew up and expanded my horizons, I would find myself saying things like, "I've always wanted to take a yoga class." Several years ago, my coach said to me, "You know Karen, what you seek is seeking you." Mic drop. Wow. That just made a whole new world open for me. To me, it meant that if you find yourself drawn to something, then connect with it! I began taking classes on mindfulness and a few yoga classes (which kicked my butt). I found that when I took time for myself, it gave me more clarity on where to move forward.

Self-care can be a difficult concept to put into action. Intuitively, we know we have needs, but it can be easy to acquiesce to the needs of others. It seems this is especially the case for women, as I have seen in my coaching. We are quick to forgo sleep to ensure the clothes are folded, skip exercise because someone has to pick the kids up from soccer practice, or even postpone going back to school because there just isn't any time or money for it. When you allow these things to take priority, you are sacrificing your self-care for others.

In the facilities management world, we focus on minimizing downtime. We complete preventive maintenance tasks to ensure our equipment runs at an optimal level because we want to prevent failures as much as possible. Often, there is no discussion about investing in preventive maintenance on expensive equipment; it's common sense to extend its life as much as possible. But we aren't always successful because—even with the best maintenance programs—equipment still fails, and outages occur. When we think about our daily lives, we, too, try to minimize downtime. Yet we pack our days full with tasks, errands, and commitments.

I live past a stretch of I-45 on the south side of Houston that has been under construction for the last twenty years. My husband complains that they build the houses first and *then* expand the freeway. In some ways, we do the same thing to ourselves. We add more and more responsibilities, and then when our lives feel overwhelmed, we can't seem to figure out how to expand the freeway!

We all have experienced getting sick because we ran our bodies and minds on full RPMs and eventually just broke down, but when that happens, we're no help to anyone! Just like the air handler that needs to be shut down to grease the bearings, our bodies and minds need space and time to recover. It's a no-brainer to invest in the maintenance of a piece of equipment, but for some reason, we don't take the same approach with ourselves. It is hard to make ourselves a priority. We feel selfish to spend time meditating, exercising, or spending lunch with friends. There is just too much to do!

But actually, it's having the discipline to take time for our mental and physical care that minimizes our personal downtime and keeps us running at an optimal level. For example, there is much scientific evidence that our brains need sleep to allow for repair time, yet that is one of the first things we sacrifice. Self-care is not selfish; it's critical maintenance. Just like on the airplane, you must put on your own oxygen mask before you ensure others have theirs on. Spend time reflecting on what part of your self-care you have been skimping on and where you want to make changes. You cannot serve from an empty vessel. Rest before you are tired.

Intellectually Fit

If you spend your workday doing activities that take a lot of brainpower, you probably feel mentally exhausted when you go home. When the day is over, should you just veg on the couch and watch *Family Feud*? What if your day job is more routine and therefore not as mentally taxing, should you go home and read about tax law? The answer is that you want to exercise your mind differently than you do during the day; your mind needs diversity. Even when I was in peak running shape, doing twelve-mile runs, I often couldn't do common cross-fit exercises, such as chin-ups and push-ups—but I could belly up to a bar! Hence, the popularity (and importance) of cross training. It makes you strong *all over*, not just in a single area, such as your aerobic capacity.

Reflect where you need to in order to get your mind in shape. Do you need more crossword puzzles or novels? Less *People* magazine and more *Science Weekly*? Only you know which mind muscles need a workout.

Finding Margin

In his book *Margin*, Richard Swenson, MD, describes margin like this: "Margin is the space between our load and our limits. It is the amount allowed beyond that which is needed. It is something held in reserve for contingencies or unanticipated situations. Margin is the gap between rest and exhaustion, the space between breathing freely and suffocating." I don't know about you, but I seem to have big swings where I sometimes have zero margin and other times I have a lot of margin, such that I feel guilty just sitting on the couch! I get a big sense of, "Shouldn't I be doing something? What am I forgetting? Surely I don't have time to sit and watch bad TV?"

Where Are You on the Scale?

Where are you right now on the margin scale? On a scale of one to ten, with one being, "you have enough extra margin you can exercise, eat healthy and get eight hours of sleep," and ten being, "you're in the hospital getting IV fluids because you're dehydrated from taking care of everyone but yourself," where are you living today? This week? This month? Is where you are where you want to be? And if not, how do you move the scale?

Strategies

Of course, you can't create margin out of thin air or even those cool 3-D printers. The key is that you must say no to make room for yes. There are things I really want to do—organizations to join and events to attend—but I monitor my free time like NASA's mission control. I have to work hard to protect my margin and often have to make decisions I don't like, but I know that it's saving me from suffocating later. It's like carrying extra body weight: it's a lot easier to not put it on in the first place than to try to get it off later!

Where at work and home can you create some margin? What are you holding onto that can be delegated? What have you recently said yes to that you now need to change your answer to? Have a goal this week to find thirty minutes a day of new margin. Use it for self-care, mental care, or something physical. Pay attention to where you are on the margin scale, and ensure it doesn't creep up without your permission.

Get Out and Get Quiet

Even though my husband and I don't have children, I love to take summer vacations. I'm not sure why I choose to fight the crowds when I can go on vacation in any month, but there is something about being around younger people when they act so carefree and full of opportunity. Do you remember what that was like? When you were, say, thirteen and had three full months to just do whatever you wanted? Sleep late, stay up late, do projects, swim, read, hang out outside, and sleep over with friends. When I was a kid, we didn't take trips or go to a lot of summer camps (things were different back then), we just took in the magical experience of summer—oh, and drove my mom insane.

Each year before we escape on our summer vacation, we do a simple exercise. Since everyone has a different version of what a vacation means or what he or she wants to experience or feel at the end of the time off, I ask my husband some version of, "What is your goal for the time off?" It is always helpful for me to understand what he wants to get out of it. He may say things like, "I just don't want to be rushed or have each day programmed to the last detail," or even, "You know, I just want to have some quiet time with just the two of us." These are always great discussions because then I get to share what *I* want to get from the time away. My goals are typically different than his (the joys of marriage!) But having the discussions before we leave allows us both to understand where the other is coming from and negotiate a compromise. This is a lot easier discussion on the patio the weekend before than the morning in the hotel room arguing over that day's activities. We are trained to get clarity on expectations at work but forget to do it at home.

I am fairly rigid about taking my time off. I protect it, and I honor it. It's not just important to me; I consider it critical. It's not just "time away from the office." For me, it's also about getting out and getting quiet. Get out of your normal surroundings, go someplace, and just be in the silence. Embrace the quiet and serenity to allow your mind to rest. You hear all the time how our lives are a 24/7 barrage of "noise," so you must take some time to *create* some quiet space for your mind to recharge.

What If You Struggle with Silence and Stillness?

I, for one, have a hard time sitting still. If I'm at home, I am usually found multitasking. I'm washing clothes while emptying the dishwasher and making my next move on Words with Friends. Even sitting outside "relaxing" can be tough for me. I need to read a book or magazine or otherwise occupy my mind. I used to think it was because I am a type A personality and that my always-on-the-go attitude was just part of my personality. I have now come to realize that it was really just busy work because being still was uncomfortable.

Uncomfortable, because when you are still, there is no hiding from what is really most alive for you. The feelings are allowed to come to the surface and just be, and we—as a society—really don't allow for that. When I am still and allow myself space, this allows me time to process life. It is in this downtime that I slow down, get clarity and perspective, and often have "aha" moments. About six months ago, during one of these "time-outs," I realized it was time to write a book. It had always been on my bucket list, but I could not decide on a focus area, so therefore, I never had to start. The time to sit, think, and process allowed the clarity of topic to come into focus. Once your mind is quiet, you will hear what is "speaking" to you.

Slowing down creates clarity, provides inner power, and creates energy. I challenge you this week to slow down; create space for life to settle and for clarity to appear. This is key to know what you need in order to feel renewed. At a minimum, you need alone time, quiet time, and "me" time. With time being so precious, it's key that we create and protect our margin. And while emergencies come up and priorities change, when you don't care for your soul first, you are creating a situation that cannot be sustained. Leading by example in this area will have a bigger impact than you can image with not only your staff and colleagues but also your family.

Key Takeaways

- Self-care is not selfish. You don't have to justify or explain to anyone what you need in order to care for yourself. Only you know.
- Slowing down creates clarity, provides inner power, and creates energy.
- You must have clarity about what your needs are and how you are renewed.
- Having margin creates the space that is needed for your self-care.
- If you are experiencing downtime (sick, low energy, etc.), it's an indicator that you are ignoring your self-care.
- Say no to make room for yes.

My Takeaways

Action Steps

- Identify areas where you can make adjustments to create some margin. How much do you protect your current margin?
- Identify what renews you. Identify your mental and self-care needs.
- Assess how much self-care you are doing right now. Do you need more? What is getting in the way? Where can you ask for help?
- Identify something each week that you will do to honor your self-care. Brushing your teeth does not count.

My Action Items

_____

_____

_____

_____

_____

_____

_____

_____

_____

_____

_____

_____

_____

_____

_____

_____

_____

_____

_____

CHAPTER 3

Awareness

> If, then, I were asked for the most important
> advice I could give, that which I considered to
> be the most useful to the men of our century, I
> should simply say: in the name of God, stop a
> moment, cease your work, look around you.
> —LEO TOLSTOY, *ESSAYS, LETTERS AND MISCELLANIES*

Early in my career, my boss came up to me and said, "Karen, I have volunteered you to teach the customer service class." I was immediately excited and jumped at the opportunity. Not because of the topic but because it just sounded like fun. At this point, I had never formally taught anything, nor did I have the awareness that I liked it and was good at it. My leader saw something in me that connected the dots for her—my ability to connect with colleagues and my outgoing personality. I just thought everyone operated like that. I taught the class—loved it—and it opened up a new world for me that I was unaware of. Awareness is funny like that.

We all know the person who has an overbearing personality about whom we often lament in disbelief at the water cooler, saying, "Does she even know how she comes off to others?" What if the person being talked about is you? How would you know? At any stage of your career, you must be keenly aware of how you are perceived—positive or negative. And since it will change over time, it's a continuous exercise to seek out and understand so that you can make adjustments if necessary. In this chapter, let's take a moment to stop and look inward as Tolstoy suggests.

What Is Your Brand?

We are all familiar with Coke, Johnson & Johnson, and even the New England Patriots. When the company names are said, we all instantly think of associations—good or bad. Have you thought of yourself as a brand? Your personal brand is who you are as a person, what you stand for, and how you present yourself.

If I stopped you in the hall later today and asked you, "What three words describe your brand?" What would you say? How long do you have to think about your answer? Think about your reputation. Do you know what it is? Do you think about it? Ever? Some of you may be able to roll it off your tongue immediately and quickly continue onto your elevator speech. You may still be talking. You can stop now; I get it. I know your family history now—we're good. For others, this can be a little uncomfortable to think about, since you may have a sneaking feeling that what you want to be your reputation is not reality. It's easier to embrace delusion and think, "Well, my reputation is that I'm obnoxious, but people just don't understand my humor." Really? You're just not understood? Pay the copay, and go see a professional, please.

How Are Reputations Developed?

Reputations are developed by people observing what you do, how you act, and what you say. If you find that, as you participate in a meeting, most of the other members don't talk, it could be that you have a reputation of killing new ideas or suggestions. Your behavior in the past may have shut people down, you've spoken over them, or you've given the message, "I don't care what you think."

You build your brand by consistently "being" a certain way—being reliable, honest, ethical, present, friendly, sincere, responsible, caring, hardworking, and intentional, to name just a few.

I hope this idea is not new to you, but what if you have a reputation that you're trying to change? It's going to take some action but also time. The first thing, obviously, is to change your behavior. If you have a reputation of poor accountability because you always miss deadlines, try actually meeting deadlines! Without a change of behavior, your brand becomes set in stone, and all you're doing is providing lip service.

The second thing you need is an advocate: someone who speaks on your behalf when you are not in the room, a sponsor who knows what changes you're working on and has witnessed some of the change already. This person can help provide the message that your reputation is undergoing a transformation and he or she can help advocate to get you the opportunity to demonstrate your behavior changing.

Like Draft Day, It's about Your Character

Every April, the NFL conducts round one of the player draft. For the thirty-two teams, it's all about acquisition of talent. Coaches, general managers, scouts, and many others evaluate potential players on a number of components to decide who they will select. And the players really have no choice where they go; that's how the draft works. The teams look at not only the physical traits of the players (e.g., weight, height, and speed) but also their character (i.e., off-field issues). All that is scrutinized to ensure the team gets a return on its investment. After all, the stakes are high.

The business world, too, is all about acquisition of talent; although we do have a choice in which job we accept (thankfully), the situations are very similar. Our experience, education, and training are equivalent to an athlete's physical traits—it's pretty objective.

Either you have the certification or you don't. It's the *character* of the person that sells the deal. Getting to the interview means you have the traits they are looking for, but the interview is where the potential employer determines if the character is a fit, which can be pretty hard to do in a one-hour conversation.

You want to be that top talent—the first-round draft pick— the manager wants. If you are not landing the jobs (and you have the credentials and experience), do some self-reflection. Chances are your brand and reputation comprise the real character others are seeing.

So how do you find out what your brand really is or how your character is perceived? Well, you have to ask; the trick is knowing *who* to ask. Think about your leadership chain of command. You want to reach out to those above, below, and horizontal to your position. The people you choose should be ones who are willing to tell you both the easy (you produce high-quality work) and the hard (your brand is that you are difficult). Don't fall into the trap of thinking your brand mirrors what you intend it to be. It may or may not. You will not truly know unless you ask. This is why awareness is so important.

Receiving Feedback

At the end of every fiscal year, we report how we did on our goals for the year and begin planning for the next year. During this process, staff is often asked to provide feedback on a colleague's performance. For some people, providing feedback isn't a fun task. They worry that what they say may get back to the person they say it about and affect the working relationship; however, I am going to offer you a different perspective: feedback can be one of the greatest gifts you can give someone.

If you are authentically sharing your experience of that person—what makes him effective and where he can grow—you are helping him see a blind spot or validate the talent he is growing into a strength. This builds trust on both the giving and receiving ends.

As the receiver of feedback, you should always thank the person for his or her insight. It doesn't mean you agree with it or see it the same way, but because he or she is willing to share it with you, it is increasing trust within the relationship. Acknowledge and thank him or her for that. For me, I am a recovering feedback panic person. Depending on who the feedback was coming from, I'd either accept it willingly as the gospel truth or move to a state of defensiveness. These two ends of the pendulum didn't serve me well. After receiving some coaching and mentoring, I was able to shift my perspective, and now I welcome it—and often seek it out! I'm reformed! I take it in and then decide how I can use it in an informed way. I want to encourage you to really think from the paradigm that your feedback is a gift to your colleagues, so make it meaningful and direct—in person with the individual is the best way. Increase the trust between yourself and the other person. We are all doing the best we can with our current level of awareness.

Always on an Interview

The philosophy that I tell every person I mentor is the key concept that you are always on a job interview. Always. We all spend a fair amount of time preparing for interviews, but the reality is that you are "in" one every time you are in a meeting or are engaging with others.

As part of a leadership team, we are often assembling teams or developing a strategy for future initiatives. Here's a little secret. When we are deciding on who would be the right person to lead the project, promote into the next position, or head up the new office, we start throwing out names. The names are either dismissed right away as not being a good fit or seen as a "possibility." Lastly, we have the names about whom we all say, "Oh yeah, she would be perfect to lead that."

The way your name ends up on one of those three subjective lists is your brand. And we already know how your brand is generated—consistent actions and behaviors—hence, why you are always on job interviews. If you are prone to slip a curse word in and you work in a very formal environment, your colleagues may laugh along with you, but they are also getting a perspective of you that you can't change later. Of course, if you are out in an oil field and let a "hell" slip, it may endear you to your colleagues!

So how do I be authentic to myself and who I am but also recognize this challenge of always being on a job interview? I can tell you, as a leader, what I look for, and I don't think that I'm unusual in my perspective. First, show up on time. Basic as that is, people still show up late to meetings. That sends the message that you are more important than I am (or us, if it's a group meeting). And I'm not saying this only applies when you are meeting with someone more senior than you; it *always* applies.

Second, get along with people. Can you participate in discussions and debate topics without losing your temper? Can you help facilitate tough topics, or do you retreat (code for pouting) if you feel like you're not being heard? I know several people who can disagree but who are able to do so in a way that moves the conversation forward. If you get the reputation "difficult to work with," your job interview is over.

Lastly, follow through. If you say you're going to do something, do it. This is so simple, yet so many people can't seem to do it. So often, people follow through when they commit to the boss, but they don't when they commit to a colleague. Hence, the concept "you are always on a job interview!" Someday that colleague may be on the interview panel judging you, and he or she may have a very different perspective than someone else.

Yep, that's the magic. Show up on time, learn how to get along with people, and follow through. When we sit around the table and run through the names of potential leaders for the project, those are the first three gates you have to get through, and if you can't do that, you'll stay right where you are. After those three, we then look into experience, knowledge, and so forth, but failure on those three basics won't even get you to the table.

Finding Your Leadership Voice

> When you engage in a work that taps your talent and fuels your passion—that rises out of a great need in the world that you feel drawn by conscience to meet—therein lies your voice, your calling, your soul's code.
>
> —STEPHEN COVEY

I tend to have a quick wit. Often, when it feels like a meeting or social setting is getting a little heavy or tense, I will share a comment or make a joke that will break the ice. When I was first a manager, I did not do it very often until I became comfortable with everyone in the room, wanting to make sure they knew me and my humor.

Now that my leadership style has fully developed, I hone this talent. What may seem like just a personality trait has become a key component of my leadership voice. I don't suppress it or hide it, whether or not I know the people around the table. It allows me to get others to relax so ideas and solutions can follow. Once I was aware of its power, I embraced it and have learned how to leverage it.

When we first enter the workforce as young professionals, we all tend to look around to find a role model—male or female—whom we relate to or want to emulate. We notice their demeanor, style, and most importantly, how they dress for success. This is especially the case if you enter a male-dominated field like construction. You are trying to figure out the balance of fitting in and establishing yourself while not losing the essence of who you are. If you're not careful, it is easy to slide into the trap of mimicking others who are successful instead of finding your own voice.

The reason it can be an easy trap is because stakes are high. This may be your first job; you may be joining an established team, and after all, you have a car payment to make! What can you do to jump-start the process of finding your authentic leadership voice? The key is to know yourself completely.

Voice Lessons

National politics is a source of pain for me. Often, I find myself in an uncomfortable situation in that I have a different opinion about political topics than do the people I'm around. And since we are taught, generally, to avoid politics and religion, I come to a crossroads: when to speak up and when to let it go. And since I don't like negativity (it literally has a physical effect on me), I have settled on just staying quiet. And while that helps on one front, it also hurts on another, as my voice is not being heard.

You've probably heard the phrase "silence is acceptance," which means if you don't voice your view or opinion, you are in agreement with what is being said. In the case of political talk, you may just be avoiding an argument as I am, but what about in the work setting? Does the phrase also apply? How often do you sit and listen to what is being said or proposed and not verbally acknowledge consent or challenge the premise? What holds you back from truly engaging? I'm not advocating talking for talking's sake but truly contributing your opinion or insight. When you move past any uncomfortable feelings and give your thoughts a voice, your leadership voice lessons begin. You cannot influence or inspire others if you always play it safe and keep your voice quiet.

Work on your leadership voice lessons. Consciously work to know when to speak up and when to let it go.

Personal Truth

Have you ever heard the concept *personal truth*? Up until about a year ago, I never had. I was struggling with a situation with someone; I was assuming that this person was "seeing" what I was seeing and why I was so upset. But he was not. After about a week of consternation on my part, I finally got up the nerve to speak clearly and directly about what was bothering me, but it was not easy. Two things happened. The first was that I felt better because I was acknowledging aloud how I felt about it to him and to myself. Second, it opened up a conversation about the situation instead of dropping hints or avoiding it.

Personal truth is simply what is true for you: how you feel about the situation—your perspective of what you are seeing and, more importantly, experiencing. And, only *you* truly know your perspective, which is why it's called personal truth. Others may think they know what you are experiencing or provide their commentary about the situation, but the reality is that it's clouded by *their* personal truths. It can be difficult to express if the topic is a touchy one or if there is a history of discord between parties.

So then why deal with it, and how does it play into awareness? If the relationship is important to you (e.g., a family member) or to a goal you want to achieve (e.g., a work project) then expressing your personal truth is essential to build and grow trust between you and the other person(s). It doesn't always mean the other person will change his or her behaviors or actions, but giving your feelings a voice is key to any relationship. If the other person doesn't change, then you can decide how to proceed, which puts you in a position of power not that of a victim. Having a keen sense of personal awareness about how you are feeling and then taking action to work through it is building a key leadership muscle. As you get more comfortable expressing what you are seeing and how you feel about it, you are behaving in a way in which we need all leaders to behave.

Dig Deeper

Everyone has seen pictures of the Caribbean sea. The clear, blue water is the envy of many avid scuba divers. Most of us who swim typically play in the top six to eight feet of water; scuba divers—with the right equipment and training—head to thirty, fifty, or even eighty-plus feet to see sights that can only be experienced at deeper depths. The water is also different at those depths, usually several degrees cooler as you go past the thermocline (which is the region in a body of water where there is an abrupt change in water temperature).

With that metaphor, think of who you want to be both at home and in your career. As you reflect, you are playing in that top six to eight feet of water. It is what you know and what is most comfortable for you—surface thinking. But true transformation happens in the deeper levels. And like scuba divers, you need some extra equipment—which is what this book is intended to help you with.

Get yourself a journal and spend some time going into the deeper water. Ask yourself, "What about my career is deeply important to me?" Write for several minutes on that question alone. Then reflect on, "What is it that I'm being called to?" After several minutes on that question, ask, "What matters most about this? What are my feelings about this?" Continue swimming down, uncovering the beauty of your inner soul. This is not fast work.

When you have spent some significant time on those items alone, then ask, "What possibilities are there? What are the possible action steps I want to take on this topic? What is the way forward for me?" After scuba divers finish a dive, we fill out our logbook—which is our journal to record the dive in all its glory—both the good parts and bad. Begin a logbook of your journey—don't be satisfied with just a snorkel; take the risk to swim deeper.

Putting It All Together

If you are not aware of how you are seen, perceived, and viewed, it hinders your ability to grow and advance as an individual and as a leader. While feedback may not always be easy to hear, it may be just what you need to redirect your actions and straighten your course, or in some cases, point you to a new industry or career field. Both outcomes are good. You have to consistently find time to stop and evaluate how you are seen by others.

If you find that how you are seen is not in alignment with who you are, then you have some work to do. Before you charge off to correct things, spend some time journaling to truly understand what you want to represent and what is important to you.

The power you own is that there is only one of you in this world. Because of that, you have a unique leadership voice. To develop that voice, you must have clarity about who you are at your core. This deep reflection takes work and willingness to receive feedback that isn't always pleasant. However, the harder you work at it, the more natural and effortless your leadership voice becomes. These first three chapters are just the beginning. You change over time, and your values and priorities shift as your life evolves. Because we affect so many others in our lives, understanding ourselves is the most worthwhile journey we can take.

Key Takeaways

- Have a high degree of personal self-awareness.
- You have a brand. Find out what yours is and determine if it's what you want it to be. If it's not, make adjustments.
- Actively and continually seek feedback.
- You are always on a job interview: show up and deliver, regardless of the audience.
- Journal to uncover your deeper desires about the impact you want to have both at home and at work.
- Knowing yourself completely allows you to lead authentically. This, in essence, is your leadership voice.
- Your brand is influencing your career, so learn what it is, and make changes if you need to.

My Takeaways

_____

_____

_____

_____

_____

_____

_____

_____

_____

_____

_____

_____

_____

_____

_____

_____

Action Steps

- Spend some time defining what you want your brand to be. Does it align with your values and talents?
- Seek out three people, and collect feedback on your brand. What changes will you make to align your brand with your values?
- Do a self-assessment on the three simple efforts of showing up on time, getting along with people, and keeping commitments. Do you do them? Really? Or are you already working on justifications as to why not?
- Where do you need to go back and "clean up" some of your actions that don't align with your brand?
- Journal to uncover more layers of what drives you and why. How do your answers align with your values?

My Action Items

_____

_____

_____

_____

_____

_____

_____

_____

_____

_____

_____

_____

_____

_____

_____

_____

PART II

It's about Others

Once you begin to have clarity about who you are and what you are about, you can then shift your focus to the next phase—community.

CHAPTER 4

Don't Try to Go It Alone

Encourage, lift and strengthen one another. For
the positive energy spread to one will be felt
by us all. For we are connected, one and all.
—Deborah Day

W hen I first started my professional construction career,
there were not a lot of women in leadership roles, and
even fewer on the jobsites. There just weren't a lot of
us around where I was working. Even so, I was mentored by many
great male colleagues. However, I was always looking for someone who had already achieved the level of success I desired to
help me navigate the waters I was experiencing or give advice on
how to approach a situation. You have to keep in mind that this
was long before social networking like today, in which you can
create networks of support quickly. I always thought that if I ever
became an executive, I would ensure that I was reaching out to
help younger women professionals.

Fast-forward many years, and I found myself promoted to
a senior leadership position. A few months later, when another

woman leader joined the team, even before I'd met her, I had made up my mind that we would have an alliance to be role models to the women in the division.

After a few months, I approached her with a plan to begin our version of "Lean-In" circles. The Sheryl Sandberg book *Lean In* had just come out, and the national conversation was gaining ground in the public eye. We wanted to start a group of women who could not only laugh together but also mentor, support, and encourage one another in a way that would transform our careers. My new colleague graciously concurred, and off we went.

Initially, we assembled twelve women with diverse titles, roles, backgrounds, and responsibilities. They were women who had previously been mentors, either formally or informally, and we knew they, too, wanted to create an environment that nurtured future women leaders. We began meeting for ninety minutes once a month for a year. In many ways, we followed the kits found on the Leanin. org site, which were extremely helpful and well done.

The meetings alternated between an educational topic (such as negotiation) and exploration topic in which a member brought an issue she was having, and we explored it as a group. Like any team, it took some time for the group to form, storm, norm, and perform. If you're not familiar with that concept, it is a group development model created by Psychologist Bruce Tuckman. Each step is required for a group to grow, work through issues, and deliver results.

During this same time, as the twelve of us were just beginning to figure out what this group was about, a major reorganization in our division occurred. Coincidentally, about four of the women in our group were part of the reorganization, and their work lives had been turned upside down. New leadership positions were created, and all interested parties were encouraged to apply. In some ways, the timing couldn't have been better. The affected women had a new network of supportive colleagues, a forum in which to express their fears, and trusted friends to encourage them to take risks.

One, in particular, was hesitant to apply for a position that would have been a promotion. She knew she could do the job but wasn't sure if she was ready, how it would look if she applied, and because she knew her competition, she figured it was a long shot and a waste of time. In this moment of self-doubt, we all told her, "Apply! Hit the send button!"

"Hit the send button" was our rally cry because job applications are now, of course, all online, and while you can fill them out without risk, sooner or later you get to the bottom of the screen and have to hit the send button. She hit the send button, got the interview, and got the job. It felt like validation for the necessity of the group and its benefits. In a two-year span, several in our circle "hit the send button" and saw results, including four promotions. But it really wasn't about promotions; it was about taking risks.

Our lean-in journey was not without some bumps. While we all like to think our male colleagues understand women's situations, the fact is, most do not. Some seek understanding, but many don't. I did make some mistakes along the way. While I had support of the departmental leadership, I did not effectively communicate to my peers what we were doing and why. The result was that as questions were asked of my peers, such as "What are they doing in that meeting?" they were not prepared to respond. Initially, there was some negativity and snide comments about the program, but we moved through it all and just kept meeting, supporting one another, and "hitting the send button."

After our first year, we expanded the program. We let anyone in facilities management sign up to be placed in a circle. The original "charter" members were paired up and became the facilitators of new circles. We assembled the circles based on a few parameters. First, of course, we didn't place anyone in a circle with that person's boss. We also looked for a good mix of staff, managers, and directors so everyone could learn and be mentored by people with a range of experience. There were now five circles meeting for a year, and once again in the fall, we called for new participants and expanded the circles again.

All in all, it has been a successful program of creating exactly what we were looking for in a male-dominated industry of design, construction, and facilities management.

During this time, I attended a luncheon celebrating women leaders. I sat beside a young woman who was early in her career who, I guessed, was probably in her late twenties or early thirties. As we began to share what our professions were, I mentioned that we started our own version of lean-in circles. She replied, "Oh, I have wanted to go to one of those meetings. Where are they held?" I kind of chuckled and said, "You don't go to a lean-in meeting; it's not like AA; *you create them*." She was looking for a secret sauce, but there isn't one. Support, encouragement, and risk—it all takes time. This was her leadership moment. She knew it was needed in her organization. She wanted to have it for herself and others. It was now just up to putting the work in. We exchanged cards, and I offered to help provide guidance etcetera. I never heard from her.

She may have pursued it, but I bet she did not. When you're young and ambitious, you often fall into the trap of competition. You have a scarcity mind-set—there may only be one promotion opportunity in our company and I want it—versus an attitude of abundance. It's like leaning into a curve on a motorcycle. It seems so wrong, but yet, that is exactly what you need to do. Bringing your colleagues in makes the pie bigger not smaller.

How to Create a Support Group

Let's explore the steps to make this happen. It's not hard, but a road-map sure makes the trip to the beach better. Well, that and an ice chest.

Step One: Seek Out a Coconspirator for Your Group
I'm a huge fan of this because it will help you identify blind spots as you develop the team, but also, there is power in numbers. It doesn't become "Donna's support circle"; it becomes "Donna and Margaret have a women's coaching group." The other benefit is that if one of the founder's moves on to her next career stage, the group has a better chance of staying active.

Step Two: Talk to the Boss
As a team, inform the boss(es) about what you're doing and why. Some may be receptive and supportive; others may not understand why it's needed. Do your homework here. Know your audience, and if you need to support your plan with data (e.g., only 20 percent of directors in our division are women) or with stories. Be clear with what you want from them; make clear requests. These efforts typically don't cost anything other than time and sweat, but you want their endorsement of the effort.

If you don't get the support you need, you have an interesting decision to make. You can decide that you want to proceed with the effort and just do it off the radar (e.g., meet off-site at lunch or nights/ weekends) to help create the force of change you want to see in the organization. Or you can decide if this is really the place you want to work. Is it conducive to growing the next generation of women leaders? Only you and your partner will know the answers to these questions. But if you get just *slight* resistance, recognize that there is a reason you have the passion to do this; there is a reason you are reading this now. It's because you are already a leader, and that leader is trying to come out. Let her come out and proceed!

Step Three: Brainstorm Potential Members
Depending on the size of your company, this could be easy or hard. Larger companies are easier in that there are more women at varying levels and backgrounds. Seek out those who are already known

as mentors, formally or informally. Get diversity of education, background, industries, and personalities.

For smaller companies, this can be tricky as there may only be ten women in the whole company! Since honesty and authenticity of sharing issues are paramount, you may not be as comfortable with sharing. In that case, I recommend another option. Your support group is usually focused around a common subject (e.g., engineering, IT, etc.) so look to the professional organizations that you belong to, and create your group from there. There are typically women who are familiar with the industry, and since they are with another company, you will certainly get unbiased perspectives about your challenges. If you're an entrepreneur, reach out to chamber of commerce meetings.

You goal is to recruit six to eight, or a maximum of twelve, women who are willing to meet regularly.

Step Four: Meet, and Set Some Rules of Engagement

At the first meeting, you need to work as a group to establish a few components. It's critical that everyone shares what they hope to gain from the group. What is the group's objective? What behavior is expected (e.g., participation, confidentiality, etc.)?

How will the content of the meetings be handled? If you're unsure where to start, the Leanin.org site has a tremendous amount of information. If that doesn't seem to fit your team or style, you have a couple of options. One is to meet similarly to a book club in that you can take a current business book and discuss how the topic affects the group's members. A second option is to discuss an element of women leadership and how each person has experienced it. A third way is for each person to bring an issue she is currently working through and share it with the group. Open discussions on real situations are incredibly powerful.

In our groups, we rotated the hosting of meetings among the participants. They often would pair up to host the meeting, but this was really key in that it helped get people out of their shell and take some risks in a safe space.

And, of course, there are meeting logistics—where to meet, duration, and frequency—to consider. I recommend you start with a one-year commitment to meet as a group. We always write up the rules of engagement after the meeting and use them as a guide through the year.

Step Five: Start Meeting!

The key component is connecting with your colleagues and working to establish trust such that the space of the meetings is safe to share your fears, successes, and struggles, all without judgment. Always start the meeting with a check-in by each person: a simple touch point to see what is going on with each member, what is most alive for her, or what is heavy on her mind. While this is intended to be short, we had many a meeting where this is all we did, and it was incredibly powerful. As with any group, you will need time to form, storm, norm, and perform. So, don't expect people to necessarily open up right away; it may take a couple of months, but trust me, transformation is occurring.

Step Six: Adjust as Necessary

Like any endeavor, there will certainly be adjustments along the way. You may have people drop out or have to deal with personality challenges among the team. These types of situations provide you with another leadership opportunity. Tough conversations are needed from time to time, so now you have a front-row seat to practice!

Step Seven: Share Progress but Not Details

As the group begins to jell and members are taking risks, seeing self-growth and gaining confidence, celebrate it as much as possible! Keep your boss(es) apprised of how things are going but not about the details. It's critical that the meeting contents are confidential. You just want the boss to know that the time and effort you are all putting in are reaping rewards for the team, and ultimately, the company.

Step Eight: Collect the Data

At the end of the first full year, take one of the meetings and simply pause to take inventory of successes and how people feel they grew over the year. There are two purposes for this. The first is that you want to truly celebrate the transformations that are occurring; if we don't stop, life just keeps moving on, and we miss the opportunity to celebrate the journey. Second, it provides you the "data" you may need if you are asked by your boss about the benefits of the effort. It also lets you see progress over the coming years. Are more women applying for jobs, getting interviews, and landing the jobs? What is the individual data for your group?

Working in any male-dominated field can be tricky at first. Minimize your learning curve by not trying to go it alone. Whether you do it within your company structure or outside of it, establish a support circle of women in your industry who can share their stories, advice, and counsel in a supportive way that moves the group forward. Group mentoring is a powerful way to grow as a leader and "pay it forward" to those coming up behind you. Be the mentor you needed when you were in their positions.

Key Takeaways

- Leaders, and especially women leaders in male-dominated fields, need support. Don't be a martyr and go it alone.
- Don't wait for someone else to form a group; step up, and do it yourself.
- When creating a group, leverage the resources that exist and adjust for your circle's needs.
- Ensure that you capture objectives and goals of the support group at the beginning.
- Regardless of how long you meet, always pause every few months to gauge personal progress and capture the transformations that are occurring. This is part of the journey.

My Takeaways

_____

_____

_____

_____

_____

_____

_____

_____

_____

_____

_____

_____

_____

_____

_____

_____

_____

_____

Action Steps

- Determine if you would benefit from group mentoring. If the answer is yes, identify a partner with whom to launch your own version of a Lean-In circle.
- Reach out to other women in your organization to gauge their interest and desire to participate.
- If you're meeting during business hours or using company resources, get approval from your boss.
- Pilot a circle to determine how it will work for you/your colleagues.

My Action Items

_____
_____
_____
_____
_____
_____
_____
_____
_____
_____
_____
_____
_____
_____
_____
_____
_____

CHAPTER 5

Personal Board of Directors

> She generally gave herself very good advice
> (though she very seldom followed it).
> —Lewis Carroll, *Alice's*
> *Adventures in Wonderland*

In chapter 4, we discussed being a part of a group support circle. Several circles had a couple of ladies start attending, but they slowly just dropped out or stopped coming. I will be the first to say that a support group will not work for everyone—and that's OK. Because we all work differently, this path may not work for you, and if that is the case, I would just offer that you have someone who can serve as your sounding board.

Not a spouse or best friend, but someone who has your best interests at heart and will tell you what you need to hear. You often hear it referred to as a personal board of directors. It is critical that you seek out different perspectives on challenges you have or decisions that need to be made. With your personal board of directors, you want to have diversity of experience, background, and knowledge.

When I first started my career in construction, my outgoing personality seemed to always result in making a lot of contacts and connections. My career moves were rarely orchestrated; they were more from necessity because a project had ended. As I got into larger organizations, my network increased, and I found that I had a few trusted colleagues whose opinions I valued, and I would often seek them out for guidance and counsel.

It's a key resource for women working in male-dominated fields. While everyone benefits from them, women in these industries often need an unfiltered perspective. Let's think about companies that have boards. The role of a board of directors is to steer the company with the sole purpose of ensuring its prosperity. They consider the interests of not only the company's shareholders but also those of the stakeholders, thinking about both internal and external impacts.

When you think of your career as a business, "You, Inc.," who sits on your personal board of directors? Have you ever even thought about it? While you may not have consciously created a board, you probably have one subconsciously. It probably is some combination of family members, friends, and colleagues or maybe someone highly invested in you, such as your personal trainer.

The reality is that most of those traditional influences are stakeholders, and their interests are personal and not always objective. Your spouse may be supportive of your best interests, but in reality, he is too close to the situation to be truly objective. It's not that he is not on the board, but you just need more chairs around the table. Approach your personal board of directors as any other design project. Spend some time up front creating the vision and defining your objective before exploring your contact list.

You may be asking yourself, why do I need one? Perhaps you have a very clear vision for where you are going and how to get there. Successful people seek support. One of the biggest things holding women back is that we don't ask for help. We may think it makes us look weak, but it's actually a secret weapon that we, collectively, tend to underleverage.

When we try and go at it alone, it takes longer, we make more mistakes, and frankly, the struggle can be exhausting. Imagine if no one ever showed you the way to get to school. You could have gotten there, but you would have taken a lot of routes that just made the whole effort longer and more tiring. Now maybe you missed math class so it all worked out in the end, but having someone guide you would not have made you a weaker student, it would have cut out a lot of needless effort.

Getting career support is much the same way. You want to work smarter not harder. Competition for top jobs is getting stronger, so why not seek out others who have already taken many of the routes and can help you get to school on time. Their business and life experiences can be a secret weapon on your career journey.

So, who are these people you should have on your board? The first consideration is diversity. When designing your board, it is critical that you have people from diverse backgrounds, experiences, and ages. When we have people who don't think like us, we get perspectives that we wouldn't have otherwise seen. One critical person who you *must* include is your future self. When you have decisions to make, ask your future self (perhaps forty years in the future) what she would say about the situation. Often, that simple question provides a great deal of clarity.

Ensure you have an odd number on your board. If you have four people on your board and two say to take the promotion while two say to stay, you may feel more confused than when you started! Having an odd number will simply ensure that an opinion, decision, or consideration wins out. Of course, you have the final decision; it is your life after all. But having clarity from your board is just another data point that eases the process.

Boards of directors for companies get compensated for their time and expertise. And while I suppose you could pay Warren Buffet for his counsel, most likely you will not have that burden. You should, however, invest in them as they are investing in you. This means meeting with them regularly (buy them a meal at the minimum!) Come prepared so the time together is maximized. Yes, you can update them on the kids, but this is a board meeting first and foremost. Have the issues well defined, provide updates, and ensure you are clear about which topics you're requesting guidance. Don't waste his or her time or become a burden.

Keep in mind, your board of directors is not static. Each quarter or biannually, review the makeup of your board. Always be on the lookout for new members and where some fresh ideas could come from.

Where Do I Find My Board Members?

Let's first start with your inner circle. Who are the people you go to now for advice and counsel? These are people whom you respect and value their opinions, and they know you, what you're about, and the goals you have. These could be former bosses, teachers, or even family members. They are people who have known you a long time and have a perspective on your life. Pick two to three from this area.

Now think of what needs you have. Do you need more guidance around business acumen, leadership development, or industry knowledge? Identify those areas so you can begin to establish the "chairs" you need on your board. The best way I have found these types of mentors is in industry organizations. When you create a network of contacts in your field, there will always be someone who is willing to help or, more importantly, know someone who has the expertise you are seeking.

I can't think of a single professional organization that doesn't include, as part of its mission, to further develop its members. Get out and get involved. Pick two to three from the areas where you need support. By now, you should have five to seven who can fill the seats around the table of You, Inc.

Once you have determined who could be on your board, have a conversation with each one asking him or her to serve on your personal board and if he or she would be willing to be a resource for you. Provide the context of why you selected him or her, and—if the person agrees—establish your expectations (how often to meet, the type of counsel you're looking for, etc.) Creating conscious relationships is critical to the success of the relationships.

When you have the initial meeting with your board members, it is best to have a clear goal of why you need them as resources. Are you working on a long-term goal that will require regular meetings? Or do you want to have a more ad hoc relationship such that you only call on them when you need clarity? Provide an agenda with any supporting information prior to the meeting.

One area that cannot be overstated is to remain open to their suggestions. You sought a diverse group so that you would get diversity of ideas, so keep your mind open! Your advisers are sharing their insights and perspectives based on what worked for them. Often, it will resonate right away; other times, you will need to reflect on what you have heard. Only you know in your soul what is best for you, but ensure that you are keeping your eyes and ears open for a new paradigm because that can be where the magic happens. Instinct is a powerful thing, but just make sure it's not fear in disguise.

As you progress in the relationships, always acknowledge the input and time they have given to support you. You want them to feel appreciated as they have an interest in seeing you succeed.

Decision Point

At one point in my career, I was leading a fairly large team and was truly enjoying the work. I learned about a position at another hospital. They were about to undertake a significant construction project.

The exciting part for me was that it would also involve creating a department—establishing the structure, framework, and culture of a new team to achieve a strategic goal.

The only catch was that when the project was completed in three years, there was no guarantee that I would have a job. Some people don't mind that type of risk, but I'm not one of those people. I interviewed and was offered the job (I consistently tell people: *always* interview. You don't have to make a decision until you are offered the job, so it's risk-free!).

Now that I had all the details (scale, scope, money, and parking location), I leveraged my board of directors to help guide me. I talked to my dad, my husband, my former bosses, and peers to the position. Trust me, everyone had his or her opinion on what I should do. While I ultimately did not take the job, I learned the power of having a board on standby.

We all hope to have a long and successful career (however we define that), but a long career is never navigated alone. Having a board of directors creates the relationship structure to help us navigate our paths and provide an objective view of our obstacles.

Key Takeaways

- You need a personal board of directors that can be a resource for you and ensure that you prosper.
- Ensure that your board is made up of individuals who have diverse background and experience.
- Be clear on your needs and expectations for and from your board.

My Takeaways

_____
_____
_____
_____
_____
_____
_____
_____
_____
_____
_____
_____
_____
_____
_____
_____
_____
_____
_____
_____
_____
_____

Action Steps

- Identify areas in which you need a resource.
- Identify your potential board members.
- Join professional organizations to identify potential resources.
- Hold an initial meeting with each board member. Provide clarity of what you will need from each and how often.
- Meet regularly with your board members; provide updates about your progress.

My Action Items

CHAPTER 6

Mentors and Coaches and Sponsors—Oh My!

Every great achiever is inspired by a great mentor.
—LAILAH GIFTY AKITA

A few years back, I was reading Peter King's "Monday Morning Quarterback" column. In it was a section about Mickey Corcoran—a mentor to Bill Parcells (the great New York Giants coach)—who had recently passed away. Corcoran was a former coach of Parcells and was also a player for Vince Lombardi. Parcells was noting the best piece of advice he had ever received was from Corcoran.

That simple statement got me thinking, "What is the best piece of advice I have ever received, as an athlete, employee, or daughter—or in any role, for that matter?" Not simply a saying or phrase (i.e., "golden rule") but actual advice or counsel that sticks with me to this day. My mom had the classics, such as, "Always meet new people at parties," (sound advice). My dad said, "Engineering will be a good field for you to enter for the future," (which, clearly, I didn't listen to) or "You should look at attending Texas A&M," (good counsel!).

Former bosses have given me advice on how to handle specific situations, but what about long-term, overarching advice? I have really sat with this awhile now. I even asked my husband about the best advice he's ever gotten. His answer was, "Think before you speak"—yeah, he was no help as I usually don't heed that advice, either. So, this is what I've settled on. The best advice I've received was from my fifth-grade English teacher, who said, "Always strive to be a student of something and a teacher of something." That is an anthem that I often gauge my life against. Am I stretching myself to learn something new? Am I sharing my knowledge, skill, or talent with others and giving back?

It doesn't always have to be something big and earth-shattering in order to meet those goals. If I am honoring those two elements, then I have a sense of fulfillment. And when I'm unbalanced or stuck in a rut, it's most likely that I'm either not receiving knowledge (slow down and get curious) or not sharing knowledge (shift to servant mode). I return to this phrase over and over.

Most often when people use examples (as I just did with the example of my dad), they are sharing attributes of a mentor: a person who gives advice. However, mentors can be confused with coaches or sponsors. And while there are distinct differences, they can also overlap. For example, you may have a sponsor at work who also provides you occasional mentoring. Or a mentor who uses coaching skills in helping you determine your path forward.

Mentors and Sponsors and Coaches—Oh My!

It was during a time of significant organizational change that several staff members came to me asking for advice during the transition. And while I have no problem talking and giving advice, this time it was different. Stakes were higher. Colleagues were looking to me to give them sage counsel to know how to navigate these rough waters. And while at first it was fine, I soon felt as though I needed some additional skills to best help them.

Several months before, a friend had shared that she had recently gotten her coaching certification. I was immediately intrigued by this concept of "coaching" but really knew nothing about it. We all have heard of mentoring, but now there is coaching and even sponsoring. What are they, and what do I need?

Coaching

Even the most skilled and successful athletes have coaches. Even at the height of his success, Tiger Woods had a swing coach and a putting coach. Athletes have recognized for years that even if you are good at something, you can always get better, and the way you get better is with a coach.

A coach is someone who is not in your industry and who provides you specific feedback or skills knowledge to help you achieve your stated goals. He or she is a guide on the side, not the sage on the stage (which is more like a mentor).

The concept of coaching in the nonsport context has many facets. Just as there are many diverse fields of law, there are almost as many in coaching. For purposes of this book, I talk about only two areas as both can benefit you immensely. The first type of coaching can be categorized as "life coaching." Life coaches partner with clients to bring about clarity and alignment in their clients' lives. Coaches don't provide the answers; they ask questions of the client and reflect back what they hear and observe from the client. Life coaching can be immensely powerful, as the coach will challenge the thinking of the client and hold him or her accountable.

Another type of coaching is categorized as executive or leadership coaching. In this arena, coaches help clients further develop specific skills, such as negotiation, influence, or change management. In this context, coaches function similarly to coaches for a baseball team. They help prepare you before the event, maybe even observe you in action, and then debrief the situation to deepen the learning. This type of coaching can be effective for you at any level in the organization, whether you just became a leader or are ready to move to the next level.

One item of caution when looking for a coach: Just because someone can hang a shingle outside of a door and call himself or herself a money manager, you wouldn't trust your money to this person without making sure he or she has appropriate credentials and experience, right? At least I hope you wouldn't. It's the same with coaches; anyone can call himself or herself a coach, but few are actually certified. Do the extra homework to ensure the coach you are considering hiring is certified by the International Coaching Federation (ICF).

The ICF sets the global standards for the coaching industry by establishing core competencies and a code of ethics. It ensures that coaches meet strict criteria of continuous education and requires recertification every three years. Find a coach in your area by going to the website at CoachFederation.org. There are also resources for you there, such as sample interview questions. It's key that the relationship between coach and client works well for both parties.

Have a coach in your personal board of directors. You don't necessarily need him or her full time, but there will be situations in which you will want and need the services of a coach for a couple of weeks or several months.

Mentors

We have all heard of mentors, but there is much confusion about the difference between a mentor and a coach. A mentor is someone who is already successful in your specific field or industry. You seek out a mentor to ask for his or her advice and counsel. Coaches do not provide advice and counsel—mentors do. You might ask a mentor about a career decision you need to make or ask her opinion on how to handle a particular situation. In all cases, mentors are giving you their opinions and sharing what has worked for them or the lessons they have learned.

Mentor relationships can be formal or informal. In a formal mentoring relationship, you might establish duration for the meetings (e.g., once a month for one year), goals (e.g., improving emotional intelligence), and track progress toward the goals. Or they can be informal in that you reach out to your mentor on an as-needed basis. Mentors can be sounding boards who help us flesh out options to our challenges. But also, recognize that, with informal mentoring, you want to acknowledge the relationship and ensure your mentor is comfortable with the relationship as you envision it. You don't want to call this person once a week for advice only to discover that the mentor doesn't know why you keep calling him or her and ends up changing his or her number!

The need for a mentor should not be a new idea to you. What is new is understanding the kind of mentor you select. There are lots of different ways to determine the right mentor for you, and it depends on what you're looking for and need. I like to have three to five mentors at any one time on whom I feel I can call for guidance. The first thing I look for is someone who is familiar with me, my current role in the organization, and where I want to take my career. I look for someone who will be candid with feedback—and trust me, this is harder to find than you'd expect.

Another type of mentor is one who is focused on career advice. These are the people whom you admire or who are in leadership positions that you aspire to. You seek out their counsel to inform and guide you when it comes to career decisions. Their feedback is based on their experiences and lessons learned.

You can also have a mentor who serves as a sounding board. This person provides advice on handling specific situations—whether personal or with the staff you manage. Having this type of mentor is crucial if you are a new manager or leader. One of my bigger mistakes was leveraging my boss as a mentor versus a neutral, third party who could provide counsel without a vested interest. Some bosses can do that, but most cannot.

Sponsors

Sponsors are advocates who help you get the exposure you want. They vouch for you and give you opportunities to be seen and perform. Think of when a person running for president selects his or her vice president. The nominee is saying, essentially, that he or she believes this person can do the job if he or she cannot. That is a pretty powerful statement by a sponsor.

I was blessed with a sponsor early on in my career. I had been a successful construction project manager who consistently delivered projects on time and on budget. My former boss left the group to head up a new department. He reached out to me and said, "You need to apply for the supervisor position." It kind of took by breath away. I had only managed contractors, not direct reports. But before me was someone who knew the quality of my work and, more importantly, believed in me and saw potential that I didn't see. I applied for the job, but still he (and I) had to convince the department head to take a risk on me for this entry-level supervisor role. He stuck his neck out for me and took a risk. I got the job and have, ever since, been immensely thankful that I had a sponsor during this key point in my career.

What do sponsors do for us? They advocate, connect you to senior leaders, focus on career opportunities, give you tips about hot jobs, use chips on behalf of protégés, and help expand career visions. Sponsors may help advocate for you for the next promotion, call in favors for you, and expand your expectations of what you can do. Most importantly, they make connections to senior leaders and advise you on executive presence (e.g., polished, poised, and professional.) They may take you to their meetings and have you shadow them—but you shouldn't be washing their cars!

If you have a sponsor, what is your role as the protégé? Because the sponsor is sticking his or her neck out for you, how you act is a reflection on him or her. You must show loyalty, demonstrate trust, promote the sponsor's legacy, and last, contribute 110 percent. Sponsors will only take on a proven performer. A sponsor wants someone who can be trusted and who promotes his or her legacy as a leader and a developer of new talent.

How do you find a sponsor? They can be as hard to find as a four-leaf clover. First, look around above you in your chain of command. Who has a reputation for helping grow staff? With whom have you worked directly who knows your abilities and reputation? Where do you want your next job to be, and whom do you know in that leadership chain? If you don't know anyone yet, who can introduce you? You may have to network to find a sponsor who will work with you. Once you've identified a potential person, have a meeting with him or her to make the request. What are you looking for in a sponsor, and is he or she willing to partner with you? What can you each expect from the other? How long will the relationship last? The sponsor-protégé partnership can be one of the most powerful ones of your career.

As you move through your career, you will need coaches, mentors, and sponsors. And all can and should serve on your personal board of directors and be resources for you. Spend some time reflecting on where you want to go in your career and where you need more knowledge or skills. From whom can the help come, and is it needed for the short term or long term? Diversify your support team in type, tenure, experience, and perspective, and once you have them in place, lean on them.

Key takeaways

- A coach helps you uncover for yourself the direction and action you want to take.
- A mentor provides his or her advice and counsel.
- A sponsor helps advocate for you to others in the organization, increasing your visibility and opportunities.
- Strive to include some of each on your personal BOD, and mix them up over time to keep perspectives fresh.

My Takeaways

_____
_____
_____
_____
_____
_____
_____
_____
_____
_____
_____
_____
_____
_____
_____
_____
_____
_____
_____
_____

Action Steps

- Do a self-assessment on what support you need to develop as a leader. Do you need a mentor, coach, or sponsor—or all three?
- Identify in which areas you could use a mentor. Brainstorm a list of possible names of those both in your industry and outside of it.
- Consider getting a coach, especially if you are taking over a new group, joining a new company, or are taking on a major initiative.
- If your goal is to advance in your current company, who can be a sponsor for you? Reach out to him or her, and begin the conversation.

My Action Items

_____

_____

_____

_____

_____

_____

_____

_____

_____

_____

_____

_____

_____

_____

_____

_____

CHAPTER 7

Every Connection Can Be Powerful

> We cannot live only for ourselves. A thousand
> fibers connect us with our fellow men; and among
> those fibers, as sympathetic threads, our actions
> run as causes, and they come back to us as effects.
> —Herman Melville

> We are like islands in the sea, separate on
> the surface but connected in the deep.
> —William James

I f there is one thing I know about myself, it's that I enjoy people. If you don't want me to know about your hobbies by the second stop, don't ride in an elevator with me! I like meeting people and learning about their stories, and I find I can always learn something. I approach conversations from a perspective of curiosity: I might learn how the life-safety code applies in this situation, where the best Mexican restaurant is in the area, or simply, what I can learn from you, which was exactly the situation I found myself in when moving from a small organization to the largest one in the Texas Medical Center. Every connection we make—both personally and professionally—affects us, whether we see it or not.

First Stop: Galveston Island

My journey into health-care facilities management was a meandering path and somewhat unusual, but looking back, I see how every connection was powerful. When I first graduated from Texas A&M University with a degree in construction management, I did not have a long pedigree of construction experience. Most of my male colleagues spent their summers working for construction companies and already had connections where they wanted to work after graduation.

I, on the other hand, had completed an internship at a construction company, but all my other experience was working at a bookstore. But by the grace of God, I got a job working for a private, custom-home builder in Galveston, Texas. Essentially, I was running his office, ordering materials, estimating, and overseeing payroll. It was a great entry-level position in a small town.

As a "people lover," I knew everyone at the city permit office and the majority of subcontractors on the island. Our company also had a woodworking business, so we were often a subcontractor to commercial contractors around the island, and again, my network was pretty big. However, when the construction economy slows, it usually hits the homebuilding industry first, and of course, small, privately owned companies are the very first to feel it.

Since I maintained the company books, I knew how many more weeks I could expect a paycheck, so I began exploring options. Back in the early nineties you didn't go onto LinkedIn or Monster.com; you did it the old-fashioned way: by making phone calls to people you knew asking for leads.

Pasadena and Bayshore Hospital

This is where my first major break came. A fellow contractor in Galveston who specialized in commercial work had a friend who worked for Bayshore, a one-hundred-bed hospital (which is considered small) about thirty miles away in Pasadena that was in the middle of a significant construction project. They were renovating inpatient rooms and the emergency room and adding a labor and delivery wing to the hospital. It was a $30 million renovation, and the director of facilities had a staff of only twelve, who were struggling to do their day jobs while supporting the contractors' needs at the same time. They were overwhelmed and needed a project manager to coordinate between the general contractor and the hospital.

Though I didn't have any commercial construction experience, the director of facilities took a chance on me based on the word of his good friend, who knew my work ethic. It didn't seem like much at the time, but looking back, I see what a leap of faith they all took with me. I worked at the hospital for eighteen months, and it was the best learning laboratory I could have asked for.

When you work for a small entity, whether it's a hospital, a startup, or an engineering firm, the blessing is that you often end up filling a lot of different roles. At this hospital, the telephone technician was a department of one. The department of environmental health and safety (EH&S) was only three people.

My role as the owner's construction coordinator also had me as outage coordinator, activation manager, move coordinator, drawing reviewer, customer liaison, and room-number assigner—just to name a few. When you work for larger firms, there are often specialists for each of those areas. It's like playing football in a small town; not only do you play multiple positions, but you often play both offense and defense. When you play football in a large 6A school (1,521 or more students), you might play linebacker, and that's it; you are a specialist.

In a short amount of time, I was able to gain great experience and exposure to many facets of both construction and facilities management. The superintendent of the construction company took me under his wing, and many of the leadership styles he taught me then, I still use today. For example, anytime we would get an e-mail about a problem on the project, my first reaction was to e-mail him so he could research the issue and respond. Well, that lasted about two days. By the third e-mail, he showed up in my office and said, "Come on. Let's go for a walk and see with our own eyes what the issue is."

Off we went to the mechanical room to really understand why the mechanical contractor was having an issue with the installation. What he was teaching me was "seek first to understand before you seek to be understood." Most of us know that as habit number five from *The 7 Habits of Highly Effective People* by Stephen Covey. But when you're twenty-five years old, you think they are just trying to avoid answering the e-mail! This was another important connection for me that continues to shape the leader I am today.

While we were under construction, The Joint Commission was scheduled to come do its triennial inspection of the hospital. The Joint Commission is the primary accreditation agency of hospitals, and an unsuccessful inspection affects a number of issues, primarily the ability to get reimbursed by the government. Back then, in preparation for the survey, facilities staff prepared a document called the "statement of conditions," which documented the status of your facilities—both the good and the bad.

The director of facilities management handed me the binder and said, "Here, why don't you create the statement of conditions?" I couldn't comprehend what he was asking me to do. I really didn't even fully understand what the document was, and he just said, "Read up on it, fill it out to the best of your ability and knowledge, and then I'll come help you finish it up." Needless to say, even for a small hospital, this wasn't an easy task, given that I didn't even understand what the task was! As I look back now, it was another moment in which someone was teaching me how to grow. The connection with the director who threw me in the deep end of the pool taught me that I may struggle, but they would not let me drown.

Heading to the Big City

It was during this time at Bayshore Hospital that I worked closely with the environmental health and safety (EH&S) team and, in particular, with one gentleman James (not his real name.) He did all the fire and life safety support for the hospital, and frankly, I didn't like him. I'm not sure exactly what it was, but he just wasn't my cup of tea. I was always cordial and professional, of course, but I didn't hang out with him much. One day he came to work and said he was resigning his position and going to work at MD Anderson (MDA) in the Texas Medical Center, and he casually said, "You know, you should look at their website because they need project managers, too." I had no idea.

Even though I went to a large college, I was still a small-town kid. Galveston was a small town, and the hospital in Pasadena was another small town. I had never been to the Texas Medical Center and really didn't even know much about it other than that there were a lot of hospitals there. Since the position at Bayshore was basically created for me, I didn't realize that other hospitals had the same need. He opened my eyes to think bigger and to all the possibilities that come along with that. The project I was coordinating was coming to completion, and there would not be a job for me when it was done, so the timing was perfect. I applied for a project manager job and got an interview.

At the time, MDA had about eight thousand employees, and the facilities division had about seven hundred employees, six of whom were project managers. Because of the amount of construction work going on all the time, a project manager at MDA had to be able to get along with a variety of leaders in the facilities organization, so to that end, I interviewed with not only the hiring manager who was the executive director of the design and construction team but also the executive director of the facilities team and the executive director of environmental health and safety. It felt like the senate hearings on a Supreme Court justice nominee! And similarly, all stakeholders needed to sign off on my hiring.

The lone holdout was the executive director of EH&S. He just wasn't sure about me. So, what did he do? He called his most recent hire who had worked with me at the hospital in Pasadena—James. Yep, the same guy I didn't even like ended up vouching for me, which led to my getting the job, and ultimately, to a career beyond my wildest dreams. I didn't even find this out until several years later.

It was then that I realized the power of connections. To have someone that I didn't even think much of have such a powerful role in my career is crazy. But as you probably already know, situations like this happen all the time where people behind a curtain are influencing your career and opportunities without your even knowing about it.

The first years in my career were punctuated by key connections, and my reputation resulted in people either taking a chance on me, investing in me, or standing up for me. I didn't even realize it was happening at the time, but it absolutely is how the world works. When you work in predominately male-dominated industries, it is even more critical that you are nurturing the connections and ensuring that you are working as much on your reputation as you do on your education.

Key Takeaways

- Be aware that every connection you make has the ability to affect you, whether you realize it or not.
- Keep every relationship professional, whether you like the person or not. Don't share your personal feelings about another colleague; keep the language focused on the product or service.
- Your reputation will often dictate unadvertised opportunities. Ensure that it is what you want it to be.

My Takeaways

_____
_____
_____
_____
_____
_____
_____
_____
_____
_____
_____
_____
_____
_____
_____
_____
_____
_____
_____

Action Steps

- Reflect on your own career to date. Can you identify which connections had an impact on your career?
- Which connections have gone stagnant that you may need to revive?
- You don't want to wait until you need a job to engage with your network; what can you do now to get reengaged?

My Action Items

_____
_____
_____
_____
_____
_____
_____
_____
_____
_____
_____
_____
_____
_____
_____
_____
_____
_____
_____
_____
_____
_____

CHAPTER 8

Share Your Stories

When you stand and share your story in an
empowering way, your story will heal you
and your story will heal somebody else.
—Iyanla Vanzant

When we suffer in silence, we think that we are
alone, different, and separate. When we share our
stories of suffering, we find that we are the same.
—Vironika Tugaleva

I had been working as a manager for about three years. I loved
my job, my boss, and the team I worked with, but I also felt as
if I was ready for the next step. A director position came open
in our department. It would involve working for my same boss and
leading not only my current team but also an additional group. I felt
like it was karma! I approached my boss and shared my interest in
the position. He stated that he wanted an engineer in the position
and wouldn't consider me because I wasn't one. I was devastated.
For about four months, I was in a fog. A door had been slammed
shut. My heart was broken because it felt like the family I loved had
rejected me. Now, I tell people that the moment it happened, it was
the best gift I could have ever received.

What my leader was essentially telling me was that I would rise no further in his organization—regardless of how good I was—because I didn't have a specific background that he valued. Once my ego healed, I realized he saved me a huge amount of time. I shifted my paradigm and began to search for my next opportunity in new groups. If he had not told me, I might have stayed working in the group several more years until another job came open. Many people stay stuck in a comfortable position because they don't ask for honest feedback about their future in the organization.

I often share that story with colleagues who just got passed up for a promotion (or even when they are applying for a promotion). The best thing that can happen sometimes is to not get the job because it can force you to look beyond what you are currently seeing.

When our Lean-In circle first started meeting, we implemented an exercise that seemed simple, but it was very powerful. When it was your turn to host the meeting, one of your action items was to share your leadership journey. Each person took a part of the meeting to share how she arrived at her current position of leadership. (It is my belief that regardless of title, you are in a position of leadership.) The results were remarkable. We all learned not only about each woman's background but also her struggles, successes, divorces, kids, aging parents, disappointments, and passions. This personal storytelling segment quickly became the best part of the meeting. But, why?

Humans learn more effectively when lessons are told in story format. When we listen to stories, we naturally listen for a connection to our own story. Sharing your personal story makes you stronger. Why do we sometimes resist sharing our journeys? We may feel our stories aren't unique or that there is nothing to learn from it. But that couldn't be further from the truth. Every person is unique, and therefore, every journey is unique. Your story may be just the inspiration that someone else needs to sign up for a class, apply for a job, or finally adopt that dog! The paradox is that when you give, you get. And when you give more, you get more. The pie doesn't become smaller; it actually becomes bigger.

The simple act of sharing your own leadership journey is incredibly powerful to the women behind you. There is always someone aspiring to be at your level (or to get the entry-level job you have). You may think instinctively, "I shouldn't tell others how I found out about this position," but that is scarcity—not abundance—thinking. But sharing your story and resources helps increase the network, and a larger network means more opportunity.

When you listen to the stories of others, you begin to pick up the unique ways each person leads, and often you can be surprised by them if you just look and listen.

After working in the construction industry for many years, I transitioned over to building management. The leader of our division at the time also happened to be a professional engineer. He also had a strong belief that in certain operational leadership roles in his organization, the positions also must be filled by engineers. Hey, when you're the big boss, you get to decide these types of things.

The result, over several years, was that the approach filtered down in the organization, and we ended up with engineers in many of the leadership positions. The danger with that is that there is not a lot of diversity of thought. In general, engineers are a unique breed. If you don't work with any engineers, just read a few strips of Dilbert and that will catch you up. As a nonengineer, it used to really annoy me because I felt like I was getting shut out of leadership opportunities, and I readily admit a small chip was beginning to form on my shoulder.

My concern, however, was that when we had so many people with one type of education, we were not becoming the strongest team possible. Which is better: Three mechanical engineers working on an airflow problem; or a mechanical engineer, a designer who spent years working for a mechanical contractor, and a former HVAC technician? I can tell you which team I want. Not everyone around every table needs to have a college degree. The challenge is getting others to look past the paper to see the talent that is there in front of them.

Leadership diversity is not simply a balance of men and women, degreed and nondegreed; it also means diversity of style. There are all sorts of leadership styles right in front of you that you may not be seeing. Let's look at an example.

An Uncommon Leader

On April 21, 2016, the music world lost Prince. Shortly after he passed, there was so much information about him in the news that it was hard to avoid it. I have to admit that I hadn't recently listened to a lot of his music, but it was the soundtrack to my high school years. The music was so unusual, both in sound and the lyrics (doves crying?) Nearly every day since his passing, reporters have pointed out so many different aspects of his artistry. I never thought I would draw leadership lessons from Prince Rogers Nelson, but here are three easy ones:

1. No matter your opinion of him, you can clearly call him a nonconformist. He pushed the envelope on what he wore, the lyrics he wrote, and the music he created. *The leadership lesson I take away from that, above all else, is to be authentic to yourself.* Only when you speak your truth and have integrity to self can you become who you were meant to be. That is powerful. I mean, he wore three-eye glasses! Talk about confidence.
2. As you know now, he was a prolific songwriter—having penned songs for many other artists. But what I really love about that was that he used pseudonyms (e.g., Jamie Starr, Joey Coco, Alexander Nevermind). He created art and gave it away. *Gave it away.* With no desire to receive credit for doing so. How often does that happen? I mean truly? *Leadership*

lesson: What are you creating and giving away to help others succeed? Or is your ego such that you want your name on the idea to be sure to get your credit for it?

3. One of the biggest reminders during the weeks after his death was how much he helped groom and mentor other musicians: Lisa and Wendy in his band the Revolution, Sheila E., Vanity 6, Carmen Electra, Susanna Hoffs (of the Bangles), and many others. He gave them a stage to perform on and opportunities to be seen, grow, and achieve success. Often the musicians were female, who at the time (late seventies and early eighties) were not given a lot of opportunity. Think about Sheila E. on percussions—we had not seen many women drummers before we saw her. *The leadership lesson: Who around us is not getting on the stage for an opportunity to perform, and what are we doing about it? Are we complaining or taking action?*

Leaders come in many sizes, shapes, and voices. Don't be fooled to think they are only in business suits standing in front of the room. They are all around us if we will look for them and embrace leadership diversity.

The Prince example tells us a lot about the power of stories. As you observe leaders and leadership qualities in others, share what you see. The stories help inspire and allow others to see a new perspective.

Influences to Your Leadership Style

My dad was a runner and great athlete, so there was a lot of physical activity in our family. I always remember being on teams: baseball, basketball, and so forth. I'm not sure why an insane coach would let a five-foot-tall person play basketball—because I was a runt. Maybe I was the comic relief, and no one told me! But I did enjoy all the different roles on the team and how each person contributed in his or her unique way. I had a high school basketball coach, Clyde Wallace, who wrote us letters before each game. The letters were part, "I believe in you," and part, "You can rise to the occasion." I still have these letters today. That experience probably had the greatest influence on me not only as a leader but also as a person. He was the first real influencer aside from my parents on what a leader does to inspire, support, push, and raise expectations.

My coaches and teachers absolutely had an influence on my leadership style and how it was formed. What are the stories you have that you know now affected your leadership style? Share them, as it will help others' and your sense of awareness.

Messiness Makes the Best Teachable Moments

I love to listen to the *WTF with Marc Maron* podcast in which he does extended interviews of comedians, musicians, and entertainers. It's a good mix as some are midcareer (forties), while others are closer to the sunset (seventies). It is fascinating to hear the very nonlinear paths their lives and careers have taken. They would work in one field, town, or industry awhile and then follow the current to a new one. Sometimes the current was intentional (following a job offer), and sometimes is was unexpected (got fired, divorced, etc.).

I find that I am absolutely captivated when the story is messy and the person authentically shares his or her mistakes and struggles. To hear in his or her own words about the difficult relationships with parents or listen to him or her laughing at the stupid thing he or she did at a job interview at age twenty-five is refreshing. The person openly shares examples of getting help, whether it's seeking counseling or living on someone's couch well past the college years. The stories are always told with a fondness for the wisdom that still affects him or her today. The artist isn't worried about others' judgments, and because it's so authentic, I find myself rooting for them.

Typically, at the end of the ninety minutes, the artist gives an approximate two-minute plug for his or her latest show or movie—which for me is a pretty good trade (eighty-eight minutes of story for a two-minute plug). All of us have a similar narrative, a backstory to the person we are today. Some of it is pretty, but much of it isn't. But it's the mess that people can relate to, and if they can relate to you, they can connect with (and trust) you. Connecting is the grease to the gears.

When it's your turn to tell your backstory, include the messy parts. Given ups and downs, downs are always more interesting. For example, after college I was an overweight aerobics teacher—how funny is that! What fool hired someone sporting a muffin top as a fitness example? But most of us can relate to a few extra pounds…so let your wall down some, and tell your messy backstory.

A Story of Bias

When women work in traditionally male-dominated industries, the topic of biases can be like walking on ice. Sometimes our male colleagues are willing and open to the conversation, and others enjoy living in denial. It's like they are truly operating in an episode of *Mad Men*. I have had men tell me, "Oh, I support your efforts because I have daughters and granddaughters and want them to succeed," but then the next day, they assemble a slate of candidates to interview for a position, and they are all white males. Nothing wrong with white males, of course, but actions speak louder than words, and their actions demonstrated a lack of commitment to diversity. It's the incongruity that drives me nuts.

Others sometimes simply don't see it, so you have to help them see it. We had a situation where a housekeeping team won a prestigious award. The management team consisted of six staff, two women and four men. Yet when the article was published, the photo was only of the four men. When the department head was asked why, the answer was, "Well, that was who we could get together on short notice."

What do you think was the unintended message? What do you think the predominately female frontline staff felt like, much less the two women managers? Certainly, it wasn't done intentionally, but without pointing out such instances and sharing why they have negative consequences, the patterns will continue.

When men's accomplishments are touted at the staff meeting, but the women's are not, what do you do? How do you challenge a peer to seek more diversity in his or her organization? I went for many years before I saw it. My favorite John Lennon quote is, "It's easy to live life with your eyes closed."

There was a hallway in our organization that had large framed photographs of influential members in our industry. I had walked the hall many times en route to meetings and always felt pride looking at the photographs because I knew these were the people who were changing the course of our history. It wasn't until many years after I had worked there that a colleague joked, "Oh, you mean the hall of white men?" Her comment took me aback. I saw the photos but never connected the dots. Surely there are women who have also made a mark. But where are they? Her offhanded comment opened my eyes and put me on a path that I would not have expected.

There are articles and books, websites and assessments that speak to this topic in great detail. My goal is not to regurgitate it for you but simply to open your eyes. Look where there is bias now in your life. Once I did, I saw things that weren't enjoyable, but at least now, I see reality. My biggest revelation was the reality that my loving, wonderful dad was chauvinistic. How could I tell? Many small things came to light, but there is one obvious one that made it clear to me. There are four kids in our family: girl, girl, boy, girl, and while all four are educated, smart, and trustworthy, he made the boy the executor of his will. Why do you think that is? I believe it was simply his lifelong conditioning. Just like the hall of white men, it sent a subtle message of how he saw the world. I love him immensely, but now it's with flaws and all.

It's important that we open our eyes and the eyes of others to see the subtle, unintentional biases that occur every day. Telling your stories of unfair treatment or biases helps open the eyes of others. But noticing it is not enough. We must also be a part of the solution by making a constructive suggestion for improving the situation when possible. Women, especially in the workplace, and even more so in traditionally male-dominated fields, are often seen as complainers or whiners, if they only point out the biases without offering suggestions as to how they can be mitigated or eliminated. I know it is not always possible, and I know men can be viewed in this way also, but we are going to focus on what we can do about the situation from our perspective. It can be as simple as suggesting a diverse interview panel. Even seemingly small steps can make a difference.

The most enjoyable movies are often ones where the lead character is faced with a tragedy. We love cheering her on to overcome the odds, rise above the challenges, and in the end, kiss George Clooney. Granted, our lives may not involve kissing George Clooney, but we do experience setbacks, challenges, and triumphs. Sharing those stories helps show others that it can be done and that we are not perfect. But most importantly, it allows others to see possibility. Learning about others' stories opens our eyes to find leaders in everyday life with uncommon styles and quiet power.

Key Takeaways

- Every leader is unique, and every journey to your current place in life is unique. Sharing your story helps the women leaders behind, around, and above you.
- When you share your story, the messy parts are the most relatable for others.
- Look around for unconscious biases that may be occurring. Share when you see them as others may not.
- Leaders come in many forms; don't be so focused on traditional ones that you miss seeing those from whom you can learn the most.

My Takeaways

_____

_____

_____

_____

_____

_____

_____

_____

_____

_____

_____

_____

_____

_____

_____

_____

_____

_____

Action Steps

- Start a stories journal; capture your biggest lessons learned along your journey.
- Look for uncommon leaders in your life. What do they do that is different and yet effective? What is unique about your leadership style?
- Speak up on a bias that you see, and make a recommendation for improvement.

My Action Items

_____

_____

_____

_____

_____

_____

_____

_____

_____

_____

_____

_____

_____

_____

_____

_____

_____

_____

_____

PART III

Now What?

This book started out by asking you to first look inward to understand yourself. As you gain awareness about who you truly are and who you want to be, the next step is to enlist help. Get help from your board of directors, mentors, coaches, sponsors, and all who influence your leadership style. And now you have information you can take to go out and create your life. You've got this!

CHAPTER 9

Go Create Your Life

> Know who you are, and be it. Know what
> you want, and go out and get it!
> —Carroll Bryant

O ne of my early coaching clients had a profound effect on me.
She had wanted to be a counselor to help youth. She loved
working around people and helping them overcome whatever challenges they were struggling with. Her father, however, was
concerned about long-term financial stability. So, at his urging, she
got a degree in accounting. She was successful but not fulfilled. Her
accounting job was one where she primarily worked alone.

Over time, she came to realize that her passion was somewhere
else. With incredible bravery, she quit her stable job. She didn't have
another one lined up, but she just knew she had to do it while she
had the nerve to do so. The actions she took provided her alignment
with her life. She is now in a career in family counseling, a field that
aligns to her values and talents. Her actions still inspire me today.
How aligned is your life, and what steps—large or small—do you
need to take to get more alignment?

Making a significant life change like my client did is a big risk.
I'm not suggesting you need to do the same; I'm just asking you
to reflect on whether your life is aligned with your values. Maybe

you like to dress in a bohemian style with flowing skirts and chunky jewelry, yet you work in a conservative environment—maybe a law office. You have to change yourself—add a filter over your image—every day for eight hours, five days a week. If you find that you have to add a filter over who you are every day, then you aren't aligned. You can adjust in the short term, but if you are not operating in awareness, the short term may become long term. In this chapter, I will leave you with several concepts to reflect on as you continue to create your life.

Taking Risks

Making any kind of change—large or small—all boils down to risk. Some of us may be risk adverse—we look to minimize it. Others may have a much higher tolerance for risk and the unknown outcome. If you want a change in your life, you're going to have to do something different. Where you are right now is the comfort zone, but transformation only occurs outside of it. I have coached many people who stepped outside their comfort zones and took risks to pursue paths that were a little scary. Each one had her own reason: one needed a loving shove; another, a mentor and guide to assist in the navigation of the new path; and still another found courage to voice what she was seeing and experiencing and owned that she wanted a different story and wanted to do something about it. It was all incredibly inspiring.

We're all familiar with the "fight or flight" instinct when we are faced with a perceived threat. For some, fear of the unknown is a threat. We would rather stay in a known average (or even bad) present situation than take a risk on an unknown future one. Fear is the fence that keeps us from changing our present situation into something we want and truly desire. We choose "flight" and just avoid confronting what is holding us back from taking the risk. Or we "fight" by complaining about the current situation, bemoaning all the outside things that we only empower by claiming that they are controlling our ability to make a change. Hogwash.

You can't leap the fear fence. Like a marine, you have to go through it, because what you truly desire is on the other side. But like a marine, you don't have to do it alone. You can leverage insight from coaches, mentors, and others who can help you see through fear and take actions—small steps toward what you truly want. Maybe it's a supervisory job; maybe it's going back to school to pursue what really makes your heart sing; maybe it's letting go of a relationship; or maybe it's running a 5K. Big or small items, we all let fear hold us back.

One of my favorite quotes is the following: "If your dreams don't scare you, then they are not big enough." Each person has that dream that kind of scares them. Let's do something about it. My challenge to you has basic three steps:

1) Write down that dream or goal you have in your mind. We all have one; write it down, and get it into the real world.
2) Tell someone about it. If this scares you, then *good*, because that means it is important to you; push past the fear of judgment and tell someone.
3) Identify three small things that can move you toward a goal that you can do in thirty days. If your goal is to go back to school, maybe it's simply to research your options. If you want to take the next step in your career, then find a mentor.
   Three steps in thirty days. Get through the wall, marine.

Listening to Instinct

Maybe you were a little stumped on identifying a goal for thirty days. I suggest that something *did* pop into your head but that you dismissed it. Let's explore that some. How well do you follow your instinct? You know, that gut reaction, first thought, and the little voice that is telling you what to do. Instinct is a funny thing in that it's like any other muscle: it must be honed—but we don't tend to think of it like that. Let's look at instinct from two angles. One perspective is when no thought or pretext exists. Think, for example, of when someone throws a wadded piece of paper at you. In a moment of instinct, you may duck your head from the wad (and then in another moment of instinct, you throw something back). It happens so quickly that your fight-or-flight reflex kicks in, and you may not even realize it.

There is also the perspective of when your "gut" is talking to you. Think of basically any police show when the police detective says, "My gut says he's not the killer." It seems that police detectives and mothers ("a mother's instinct") are rarely questioned. It is a given that their actions based on their gut feelings are accepted and are often actually asked for—"What is your gut telling you?" It's part of their professions and expected.

Do you listen to your gut? When you have a decision to make and information points one way, but your instinct says another, which do you listen to? Do you trust it? If not, how do you start trusting it? I believe that your gut instinct is a culmination of your true self in its purest sense, looking to be felt and heard in order to guide us. This is why we so often, when faced with a challenge, feel it in our body. Our stomach is upset, we don't sleep well, or we lose our appetite. (I'm still waiting for that one to manifest, as I have five pounds I need to drop.)

What if you listened to your gut instinct in the same way you dodged the wad of paper thrown at you? How do you work that muscle so you are able to take action that is most in alignment with who you are at your core (which, in turn, brings more fulfillment)? With a renewed focus, take on the persona of a police detective. Listen to your inner voice, your instinct, to feel where it is guiding you, and then take the action. Be conscious of it. Spend some time listening to your instinct muscle, so that like the detective or mom, you first ask, "What is my instinct telling me to do?" Start your own instinct boot camp.

Finding Your Art

I enjoy listening to interviews of artists (usually musicians or painters) explain how they were inspired or how they created their art. I often think, "I wish I were that creative." I have to scour Pinterest for all my ideas—from Halloween costumes, to dinner recipes, to what lotto numbers to play. And while I can play an instrument, I do not consider myself a musician. The only painting I've done was with twenty other people at a "paint party" that also involved wine. I have never thought of myself as an artist. My husband, on the other hand, can build furniture from rough sawn piles of lumber and can weld iron to create fire pits. He absolutely is an artist and has an artist's eye.

Many of us have seen people who work with their hands and know that what they are doing is a skilled craft but that it is also art. Proof of that is when you see a bad ceramic tile installation. However, my perspective is changing as, now, I am beginning to embrace the idea that each one of us is an artist; it's just that our art mediums differ. For some, it may be the dinners they create with love for their families; for another, it may be his or her ability to create a safe emotional space for patients who are undergoing treatment. What I know for sure is that whatever the medium, all art is inspired and that inspiration comes in many forms—and often without intention.

What is your art, and how do you get or stay inspired? Are you getting still long enough to let the inspiration in to hear your artist's voice? My art is inspiring people to make transformative change, and my medium varies. I may write it, speak it, or play inspirational music. For me to grow as an artist, I have to spend time to develop and refine my art. Whatever your art is, you are the only one who can create it in your voice and style. What are you doing to honor your artist's voice?

Where Are You Going?

My dad was an air force pilot and always had a keen sense of direction. I really think it rubbed off on me because I, too, seem to be pretty good at knowing where north is, where my car is parked, and although I can't see Russia from my house like Sarah Palin can, I can locate Russia on a map. And it should not surprise you that the majority of people spend more time planning their vacations than planning where they want their careers to go. Of course, I would rather schedule time for jet skiing, scuba diving, or lying on the beach, but if I want my career to progress, I need to focus the same amount of energy on the area in which I spend such a large portion of my life—my vocation.

Do You Plan Ahead or Go with the Waves?

Gone are the days of mapping out your career ladder. It's no longer a linear path, with nice, sequential, evenly spaced steps. Today, careers are like jungle gyms. We move up, down, and horizontally. Sometimes we fall, hit the ground, and have to start over again. So how do you plan where you're going if the map is constantly changing?

My answer is you have to do both. You have to have a general plan of where you want to go, the impact you want to have, and where you want to do it. But you also have to be open to being rocked by the waves. When a new wave crest comes—a new opportunity that can lead to something bigger—you have to take the risk. The wave may take you up or down, but it also may lead to an opportunity that you currently can't see. You just want to make sure you're swimming in the right location to begin with. Don't be tempted by a promotion in a field that no longer excites you.

After you plan your trip to Cancun, spend some time planning your career. Ask yourself: Where do I want to make an impact? Am I there now, and if not, what connections do I need to make to open the area up? What additional tools do I need, and how do I get them? If you're not where you want to be, start making the changes now, because the longer you stay, the harder it is to leave.

With that spirit, let's explore the impact you want to make.

Decide Your Legacy

When I woke up one morning to the news that the legendary women's basketball coach Pat Summitt had passed away, I was tremendously sad. I wasn't 100 percent sure why, since I was not a University of Tennessee fan, nor is basketball a game I enjoy watching. She died at age sixty-four, which was the same age as my mom when she'd died years ago. So maybe that was it? Lots of emotions resurfaced seeing someone go so young.

Coach Summitt was well known as a tremendous leader and role model for women so maybe that was the loss I was feeling. The more I reflected on it, I settled on the connection that Coach Summitt and my mom had both been teachers: Summitt, a brilliant, accomplished coach—and my mom, a first-grade teacher for thirty years—both had worked tirelessly to positively influence the next generation. I was mourning all of it.

In that spirit, I also have been thinking about who in my life was my most influential teacher. I've had great coaches (but I'm not a professional athlete) and band teachers (but I'm not in a rock band), but who really influenced me enough that it continues today? My first thought was my sixth-grade English teacher. I could not re-member her name, so off I went digging into the keepsake box. Do you have one of those? Mom kept all our old school stuff until at one point when I was like twenty-eight she called and said, "Come get your box of stuff; I am no longer storing it! Oh, and those prom dresses, too!" Man, kind of harsh, Mom.

In the single plastic box were all my report cards (I noted a lot of "unsatisfactory" under the conduct section), some minor crafts, and little trophies. There it was, the 1981, sixth-grade middle school record book. I scanned through the pictures of the teachers and saw Mrs. Smith (they didn't even print first names so it's impossible for me to find her now). I recalled how she shared her contagious love for stories with us. There are a lot of things I remember from that time, and I understand how it has shaped me today. I have no way to share my thanks with her, and I am just filled with appreciation for all the teachers in my life.

What can we learn from Pat Summitt? After reading several articles about her, this is what I'm taking away: believe in something bigger than yourself, demand excellence, and pursue your dreams with unapologetic abandon. What do you want people to say they learned from you after you're gone? It can be big or small. The test is: Are you demonstrating it now? It's a weird thing to think about what people will say about you when you're six feet under—but also very humbling. Spend some time this week thinking about this as it may just change your priorities. What is the legacy you want to leave behind?

Acceptance of Your Leadership Role

I'm a runner. It took me several years of running many distances before I felt I could truly own that title. And like most runners, I would track my time and distance looking to make improvements. I would average around a ten-minute mile, sometimes slower when it was hot and sometimes faster when it was cool. At the peak of my training, I did a half marathon at an average of 9:20/mile, which for me is pretty darn speedy.

Although one time I did a 5K in twenty-degree weather at 8:30/mile—but I don't count it because I was running like a crazy person so I could get back to the warm tent! Regardless, over the years my speed has gone up and down, but overall, when you look at miles and miles of my running data, I average ten minutes per mile. That is just who I am as a runner, and I am just fine with that. I accept that that is my runner's brand, and I'm happy to let people pass me without guilt or shame. But when I first started running, I would speed up when someone I thought I should be faster than would pass me. Now, I just judge the person's running outfit.

Once I accepted that, while I can make some time improvements, there is a baseline that works for me, the joy of the journey finally reemerged. It is where I am designed to be—and the data proves it. What came with that acceptance was a release. A release of self-judgment and of being critical of what I am. What things in life are you full of self-judgment about? Things like your parenting skills, your role at work, or which type of hair style really looks good on you versus what is popular? Is there an attribute about you that you're fighting—like me and my ten-minute mile? What do you need to embrace and accept so that you, too, can experience the release?

Do You Have a Toolbox or a Toy Box?

The process to obtain my coaching certification from the International Coaching Federation was a year-long one with over a hundred hours of class time. During a session, course leaders demonstrated a skill, and then we were paired up to practice it while someone listened and provided feedback on our application of it. I was new to coaching and really didn't know what I was doing. I felt so self-conscious and ill prepared to be critiqued that I stumbled fairly often.

About a quarter of the way through the class, the leader said, "Just consider this your learning laboratory. Make mistakes, stumble, and learn!" That moment changed my approach completely. I had been approaching the course like any other class in that I studied material, practiced, and then took a test to prove my proficiency. There was a test at the end of the course that I had to pass, but the course itself wasn't about linear progression. The way I became a skilled coach was by approaching the work as a learning laboratory.

Labs are all about experimenting, and when experiments fail, it is celebrated because it gives you information about what to do differently. At the end of the year, I had many techniques and methods with which to coach people. Later on, while having a conversation with my own coach, I was talking through what I had learned and said something like, "I just love having all these toys at my disposal!"

She replied, "I'm not sure you realize what you just said. Most people say, 'I have new tools in my toolbox,' but you are approaching it like toys in a toy box. Meaning, there is no wrong way to play with a toy and that thinking of the techniques in a more organic way fits the reality of life." And like that, I had another "aha" moment. Do you consider yourself to be in a lifelong learning laboratory? Do you have a toolbox (with wrong and right ways to use tools), or do you have a toy box (fluid and adjustable)? How you approach things is fundamental to the outcome.

Many years ago, I first met someone who ultimately became a great colleague and collaborator. After thirteen years, she left the comfort and security of her role to take a leap into something new. It's a real risk. It's scary and exciting all at the same time—and incredibly inspiring. She's an architectural engineer and has worked around construction projects and facilities management her entire career. But fate had a different plan for her.

It began with her being touched by a story at her church. Slowly, she began to partner with and share her knowledge and assistance with the organization. Then she made the decision. The decision to leave her secure job and join a nonprofit organization that helps child survivors of sex trafficking. It became clear where her talents and skills were calling her to be a part of something bigger. This is not a small thing, and there is no safety net. It's a decision that completely encapsulates the spirit of this chapter. She took a risk, listened to her instinct, expressed her art, and she is making an impact.

Her act of courage really makes you think. When did you take your last true risk? What gave you the courage to do it? It doesn't have to be changing a job, it could be anything, personal or professional—but the concept is the same. Are you listening to the voice in your head that wants more for you? Are you waiting for life to happen, or are you creating your life?

Key Takeaways

- If you want changes in your life, you have to step outside of your comfort zone to get them; otherwise, you'd already have them!
- Hone the skill of listening to your instinct.
- Consider what you want your art medium to be and what you want to express.
- Have a general plan for where you want to go in your career while also being open to the nonlinear path.
- Design what you want your legacy to be.

My Takeaways

_____

_____

_____

_____

_____

_____

_____

_____

_____

_____

_____

_____

_____

_____

_____

_____

_____

_____

_____

_____

Action Steps

- When you think of a goal you want to achieve in the next six months, where does your instinct guide you? Identify the goal.
- Review the goal in terms of how much of a risk is it for you. Does it make you a little nervous or scared? Good, that's what you want. If your goal doesn't, then you're not thinking big enough.
- Each week, determine just three small steps that will move you toward your goal.
- Identify what your art medium will be. How do you want to express yourself?
- What do you want your impact to be after you are gone? What changes do you need to make so that your life is in alignment with the impact you want to have?

My Action Items

_____

_____

_____

_____

_____

_____

_____

_____

_____

_____

_____

_____

_____

_____

CHAPTER 10

What I Learned about Leadership

> I want to grow. I want to be better. You
> Grow. We all grow. We're made to grow.
> You either evolve or you disappear.
> —Tupac Shakur

I remember my first job as a supervisor. I had an employee who worked at a site about two hundred miles away. Shortly after I became his supervisor, he struggled with a substance-abuse problem. I had never been in a situation remotely close to this, and compounding it was the fact that he was so far away. I'll be honest; I was struggling with the issue.

I remember losing a lot of sleep and being incredibly stressed out. I was beginning to doubt the choice I had made to get into management. I made a lot of mistakes in the way I handled the situation. And while it ultimately was resolved, I learned so much about how to work through complex situations. I wouldn't want to go through it again, but I am thankful to have had the experience. I even tell new managers now when they are in a challenging situation: you will learn more by having difficult employees than by having easy ones! Just remember, it provides you a much richer résumé. As the proverb says, smooth seas do not make skillful sailors. I'm lucky I'm a Pisces, because some very rough seas were in my future.

When I was first a manager, my mentor at the time suggested to me that if I wanted to continue to grow in my career, I would need to go back to school and get an MBA. Now, more than ever, a master's degree is needed to advance. Competition is tough, and education is often the first thing hiring managers look at to make the first cut when reviewing résumés. So, as he suggested, I went back to school—a decision I have never regretted.

Several years later, my older brother had joined the same company. We were peers in the same division. It was a nice treat to be working alongside a family member. If you think about it, most people really don't know what their parents or siblings are like at work. I always wondered what my dad was like at the office. I knew he was respected and smart, but was he funny? Did he drive change or impact in more subtle ways? We lost him early, and I regret that I never really quizzed him on his business acumen. I could have learned a lot of business savvy from him.

During a company reorganization, a new leadership position was created in the division. If I applied and got the job, it would be a significant promotion for me. I had been with the company for many years, got the graduate degree, and now the opportunity was there for me to lean in. There was only one catch. If I got the job, my brother's position would be a direct report. Our company had strict nepotism policies so the arrangement would not be permitted. Something would have to change if I got the job.

My brother and I really only had one conversation about the position when it was posted. It was cryptic and not very genuine. He said something like, "Let me know if you are going to apply for the job so I can decide what to do." I said, "Yes, I am going to apply for the job." And right then, the die had been cast. The most pivotal point in my life had occurred. I applied and was successful in landing the job. My brother never spoke to me again.

The next several years were the most horrible in my life. I had finally achieved a great position, yet I was being rejected my family member. There was pain all around.

My boss at the time allowed for my brother to report to him to address the nepotism policy, but since he and his team were part of my organization, I was having staff meetings with him sitting at the table. Let's just say it was not a comfortable situation. Staff could see the strain which made it hard for them as well. This went on, seemingly, forever. I understood why he was hurt, but I also could not understand why he didn't want success for me. As they say "It's complicated."

After nearly three years of this very difficult situation, coincidentally, leadership changed. In just a few weeks, my brother resigned. I heard that he had found a job with a large oil and gas company and has had great success there.

Ever since my promotion, I had retreated into fog. I never even got to celebrate the achievement. I avoided any and all family events. I just couldn't be around someone that rejected me.

Considering that after three years of being miserable, crying nearly nightly, I knew I had to do something. The situation was not only affecting me personally, but it was having a huge impact on my marriage. Who wants to be married to someone who alternates between being furious and depressed? It was not a fun time, to say the least. I did what many people are scared to even talk about: I saw a therapist. Inspired by a colleague at work who openly talked about her family struggles and getting help, I made an appointment.

It was along this same time that I learned from a colleague that she had received her coaching certification. I was immediately intrigued and wanted to know more. After doing some research, I chose a company to begin my training. In 2015, I began a transformation I could not have predicted. While my therapist was helping me with the past, my coaching training was helping me design the future. I learned so much about myself, my family, and who I want to be.

It's a weird situation. If it weren't for how my brother reacted and treated me, I would not have sought out help that changed my life. It allowed me to come out of my fog and start to experience my life in a whole new way. I am now pursuing new avenues, experiencing phenomenal things, and have written a book! I learned how to own my power.

From time to time, I think back to the decision I made to "hit the send button." Would I still do it if I knew how it would impact the relationship with my brother? I think so, because the journey after has been transformative. If the roles were reversed, would I have reacted the way he did? I don't believe so. Reality is that you don't know what you will do until you are in the situation.

The only thing I would change is that I would have more clarity of who I am so that I would not doubt the decision that I made. I hope you are never in the position I was in, but if so, the first three chapters of this book should provide the stable support you need.

As the fog was lifting, I began the year-long process to become a certified coach. To become a coach, you learn the skills by coaching others and being coached. Over countless hours, you begin to get clarity of self while ensuring your own alignment. It is a transformative process. At the end of 2015, I felt whole and ready to start my next chapter with awareness and clarity of my life's purpose.

During that year, I spent a fair amount of time reflecting on what I have learned about myself and the type of leader I want to be. And while I continue to grow, I have identified twelve lessons I learned along the way. I'm sure in a few years, it'll be in triple digits.

Lesson One: Ask for Help

When the situation with my brother had reached its apex, it was a horrible time for me and my husband. I was crying all the time, and he was upset because I was upset. I was on a miserable roller coaster. One week, I felt like a crappy sister and would spend days beating myself up. The next week, I would be furious at my brother for acting the way he was acting. With my parents gone, there was really no mediator.

Mental health continues to be a somewhat taboo topic. When a friend shared how she was working through issues, it allowed me to consider that I, too, could get help. One day, I finally got the courage to make an appointment. I realized that no matter where the situation was going, I could no longer live that way. I had hit rock bottom. I had never had a rock bottom before, and let me just tell you, get help before you get there because it's dark, painful, and you don't feel good—not even in your favorite outfit!

I was still so embarrassed that I had to ask for help that I didn't even tell my husband at first. I was so fearful of judgment from anyone and everyone. It would validate that I was not strong enough to manage my own life. After some time, I slowly came out of the pit. Overall, the process took about three years, and while one situation prompted it, I uncovered so much about myself and now see so much more of my past with clear glasses. Although the rose-colored ones are less painful, they held me back from becoming the true person I was meant to be.

Lesson Two: Talk about It

Having difficult conversations, confronting a sensitive topic, or expressing how you are feeling about a situation is the single most powerful thing you can do as a leader. I will be the first to admit: I am a novice at it, but I am also committed to getting better. Nothing is more annoying to me than avoiding a subject that needs to be resolved. Now I actively talk about the issues or concerns with any and all stakeholders. You will become an influential leader when you hone the skill of leading difficult conversations.

Lesson Three: Be the Role Model You Needed

Through the first third of my career, I was looking for a role model: a woman who was both powerful and approachable. One who was progressive, innovative, and emulated a sense of "I've got this." After several years of searching and not finding that role model, I made the conscious effort to be that woman myself.

I can't relive that time in my career as a young professional woman, but I can be it for the women coming behind me. Back in 1993, there was a huge controversy when Charles Barkley made a commercial for Nike that said, "I am not a role model." The premise was that he is only a role model on the basketball court and not one when he is off the court. He claimed he wasn't accountable if his bad behavior or actions off the court inspired kids to do the same; he wasn't to blame.

The reality is that you are always on the stage. You are a role model no matter who you are or your position in life. People are watching you. You are accountable for your actions and behaviors. The people who are coming up behind you, new to their career, are watching you to see how you handle conflict, how you encourage and support others, and even how you dress. Own and embrace your position as a role model.

Lesson Four: The Journey Is Long, So Stay Inspired!

I confess—I have a major addiction to podcasts. I have always wanted to explore the world of podcasts and have even subscribed to some before, but when those red bubbles would appear in the upper right-hand corner of my phone notifying me that a new podcast was ready, I would stress because I didn't like the feeling of uncompleted tasks. It seemed as if that was just one more thing on my to-do list. So, I quickly unsubscribed, and the pressure was off. Phew!

But a couple of weeks ago, I could find nothing interesting to listen to on the radio so I decided to listen to a Gallup StrengthsFinders podcast link I had received in an e-mail on the talent "arranger"—I was hooked. Hooked because my commute seemed to melt away, my mind was occupied, and I was laughing; it was the best forty-five-minute ride home in a long time.

Now I have TED Talks, humorists, and creative thinkers filling my time, and when I arrive home, I have more energy than when I left work. Crazy, right? But it makes sense if you think about it; my top talent is "learner," and my second is "positivity." So, I am learning and laughing for forty-five minutes each day, and it is filling my tank!

Podcasts may not be your answer—only you know what works for you. The key is to know how you are inspired and then to do it often.

Lesson Five: Put in the Work to Prepare

The art of making a single television episode is fascinating to me. There is so much prep time: script collaborations, table reads, camera blocking, practice runs—all leading up to the moment when the director says, "Action," and the scene is filmed. It takes several days of prep work for the few hours of filming. It reminds me of all the prep work you have to do before you paint something. In both cases, you can't rush the prep work, or you'll be sorry. I would suspect there aren't many actors among us, but who hasn't put in enough time on the sanding step only to have the paint look rough and bumpy. It can be summarized by the ratio I have heard from lawyers that, for each hour in court, there are four hours of prep time.

In this awareness about preparation, I invite you to spend some time reflecting on where in your life there is bumpy paint because you didn't prep the wood. Did you submit your résumé in haste without partnering with someone to make it great? Or maybe you went to the interview without doing any research about the company or the interviewer. Did you show up without reading any of the information prior to a meeting? Are you thoroughly vetting your idea or proposal prior to presenting it for consideration?

What recent outcomes were not as successful as you wanted? Did you put in the amount of preparation truly required? So often, others do not realize the amount of prep work that goes into a product or service so that when they try to do it, it comes out less than desired—like Thanksgiving dinner! Just ask your mom. Remember the four-to-one ratio. As a leader, preparation is critical.

Lesson Six: Be Patient with Yourself as You Are Learning

You know you don't have the patience to learn something new when your new phone has apps you haven't yet looked at, the manual to the car's navigation system is unopened, and your new husband's name just keeps escaping you! For basically all my adult years, I have been a PC person and quite fluent in the Windows world. I can put together a presentation faster than you can say "death by PowerPoint." But last year, I decided to buy a Mac, and I have to admit that it was mostly due to pressure of the reputation that goes along with owning one. Namely, that your hip, creative, and have longed your whole life to be in a cult. Where do I sign up?

So, off I went into navigating a new operating system. At first I was able to get around just fine, but slowly, my self-taught learning curve came to an end, and it became harder to complete a task in a time frame that was acceptable to me. Quickly, I was going back home to my PC to finish the document so I could get on with my life. I mean, I needed to cook dinner, fold the clothes, and protect an hour to waste on Pinterest! I was living the life of a child of divorce being shuffled between two homes, never feeling completely settled. But before I knew it, I had purchased a MacBook (because now I am totally drinking the purple Kool-Aid) and could no longer tolerate, justify, or hide my operating illiteracy. I had to find the patience and commitment to learn something new—really immerse myself in it.

Why are we resistant to taking time to learn the "how" behind the "do"? I mean, who really reads how to fully operate the car's navigation system? Isn't it just more fun to yell at the voice? I don't believe it is simply a time issue; it's deeper than that. First you have to stop swinging the bat and step out of the batter's box. The longer you have tried it on your own, the harder it is to get help. Admitting defeat shows you're vulnerable, and frankly, it can feel unpleasant.

Second, you must know your learning style. Do you want to read, have someone show you, or attend a class with others? Resist the urge to just learn a small piece instead of all the functionality.

Sometimes we jump to the easiest path (hello YouTube!), which may give only partial information and usually results in our getting stuck later because our knowledge ran out again. Last is accepting that it will take some time to get proficient, so have some patience with yourself. Avoid acting like the child of divorce like I did! Try working in smaller time chunks than what you did before, which should help keep your frustration level out of reach. Change takes patience, and patience is the partner of perseverance.

Lesson Seven: Know When to Rest Your Leadership Heart

Several years ago, I was all about using a heart monitor when I jogged. I would strap it on my chest and head out on the road. After looking at the numbers when I got home, I was worried my heart rate was staying too high for too long. Ever paranoid, I went in to do a stress test, the one where they put probes on you, set the treadmill at a ridiculous incline, and then taunt you by saying, "Go ahead; jog." Yeah, right.

I quickly went from the mental state of "I'm a running machine" to "I can't believe I had to pay a copay for this!" The technician monitored my heart rhythm, blood pressure, and breathing. And while everything was fine, it was also nice to have a baseline set of data. How does my heart operate under normal conditions as well as under stress? With the heart, we can wear devices that indicate how stressed our hearts are; it's easy to get and monitor the data if you want it.

All of us are leaders in some capacity. It may be at work leading a team, it could be at home leading a family, or it could be leading strangers to the shortest checkout line at Target. And as a leader, if you care about what you're working toward—which I assume you do—it can take an emotional toll on your heart. You expend emotional energy on your products and services.

Sometimes if you aren't careful, you stress out your leadership heart. You have a baseline leadership rhythm, pressure, and breath. A steadiness that allows you to react, adjust, and push through adversity. However, if your leadership heart has been stressed for too long, with no time to recover, rebuild, and recharge, you lose the ability to foster a spirit of community.

Where are you a leader, and how stressed is your leadership heart? Do you feel inspired each day, or do you have to work at it more than usual? How do you recover and recharge after a strenuous project or effort? Not just mentally, but by actually rebuilding your passion for what you do? Muscles grow stronger when they are allowed to rest and rebuild. Allow your leadership heart some time to breathe so you don't face plant on the treadmill.

Lesson Eight: Stay in Leadership Shape

Every four years, excitement around the summer Olympics takes over the summer. With the power of streaming all events online, many of us get to witness the pinnacle of an athlete's success. But what don't you see?

Inherently, we know that these world-class athletes spend a huge amount of time working and preparing. Runners spend hours at the track in all kinds of weather working on their craft. When they aren't running, they are in the gym lifting weights, and their diets are watched as closely as the finish line.

The athlete's body is a fine-tuned machine with the goal of optimal performance. The same can be said for professional musicians, artists, and even comedians. When you watch a performance of any kind that is executed well, hour and hours of preparation went into it that you don't see and that, frankly, you forget about. You enjoy the elegance of the performance but don't remember that these professionals probably haven't seen a new release movie in five years.

The same applies to leaders and anyone aspiring to be a leader. The "performance" is the workday. You are on stage with the objective to perform well, provide guidance, and inspire the best performance from the team. However, what is often forgotten is the not-so-fun work in the "gym." These are things like keeping up with industry trends, leadership development, and visioning.

All of these things take time, which is not easily found during the workday. So, often, leaders are found reading *Harvard Business Review* on their iPads while waiting for their kid's soccer practice to conclude. This is what you don't see. Successful leaders work on their craft all the time—just like professional athletes. They live it, read about it, and most importantly, practice it. For today's leader, this is what is required so ensure you have the passion for it before you sign up.

Lesson Nine: Make an Impact

I listened to an interview with Garry Marshall, the prolific writer, director, and actor (He gave us the Fonz!). Even at age eighty-one, he was authentic, honest, quick-witted, and very humble about his many successful endeavors. After he passed away, I read a few of the columns that outlined his rise to fame and his close relationships with many Hollywood names we know by heart. Marshall is one of a handful of people who truly influenced an entire industry.

I began to think about what would be said of me if I was gone at age eighty-one. What do I want to accomplish between now and then? It's not an accumulation of trophies or framed pieces of paper to hang on a wall. No, for me it's simply to try to affect people in a positive way. Sometimes we think we have to do something big, huge, or momentous to be remembered, but I disagree.

I often get the opportunity to speak with large groups. Although the room is full of energy, and I hope that action will follow, I really don't know for sure. But if I influence just one person, I am satisfied. She will remember me, maybe not my name or any other detail, but she will remember that that hour made a difference to her. If that occurs for just one person, it was worth my time. I know you influence your family, but outside of family, I promise you are making an impact with more people than you realize. Your words of wisdom, encouragement, and laughter may be just what they needed. And trust me, they will remember that. That becomes your impact.

I heard someone say, "I hope to peak the day before I die," and I just love that. It's my new mantra. Garry Marshall was still working just before he died. My goal in life is to keep making an impact on others up until the day I die. That, for me, will be a life well lived.

Lesson Ten: Find Your Tribe

Don't waste your time being what someone wants you to become in order to feed their list of rules, boundaries and insecurities. Find your tribe. They will allow you to be you, while you dance in the rain.

—SHANNON L. ALDER

There is much conversation that swirls around us with regard to diversity on teams. Facts and data are shared about how teams that are diverse are both more productive and innovative. I totally agree and love working on teams with people who bring diverse thoughts and approaches. I also recognize that sometimes being in a diverse group can feel isolating; especially when you sense that you're the one who doesn't "fit." And the fit can be because of many things: culture, philosophy, or even language. It's often something I talk about with job candidates I'm interviewing. It's just as important to me for us to be a good fit for a candidate as it is for the candidate to be a good fit for us. We have all worked where it felt like it wasn't a good fit for us. But what about your life outside of work—do you have a place where you fit?

I joined an organization that is part social club, part vocation club, and part inspiration club. When I got home from my first meeting, I told my husband, "These are my people!" It was just an instant feeling that I had found my tribe. It was a strong vibe that I had never felt before, and it propelled me to take on some bucket-list items. Now I'm getting some traction. I had belonged to other social groups, or vocation groups, and some were inspirational, but this one merged all three.

Are you in a community that feeds you? It could be a running club, a work unit, or even clown college. Connecting with a community of like-minded people can support you as you develop your voice and self. Being part of a community can have a unique outcome. When you're sitting with a diverse team at work, you don't feel out of place, but instead, that your voice will not be silenced. The power of finding your tribe hones your voice.

Lesson Eleven: Stay Open

I have reached the point of farsightedness so that I have to keep "cheaters" close by wherever I am. I went to the dollar store and bought fifteen pairs and have them strategically placed around the house and at my desk. I don't need a lot of "assistance," just a little. So, when I was shopping the other day, I wanted to try on a pair of pants, but the size was printed so small that I couldn't read it! And since I didn't have my cheaters on me, I proceeded to the dressing room on trust alone. They didn't fit so the dance of going back on the floor to find a new size began. It was actually all pretty funny.

The good part about bad eyesight, of course, is that it can be corrected. But the whole experience made me think about what we think we see versus reality. How often have you thought one thing about a situation but realize later that you had it wrong? What you thought you saw wasn't reality (like the *Seinfeld* episode where Jerry wasn't picking his nose, he was scratching on the *side* of the nose!). So how do you know if you're right about what you see? My opinion is simply that you don't. You must condition yourself to be open to other possibilities.

Nothing is not black and white, only shades of gray. For some people, however, that is hard to put into practice as the right/wrong litmus test is their comfort zone. Black/white situations are easier because it keeps things simple with not a lot of processing or evaluation required. (And hello, who wants to be wrong? Not me!) Yet we know intrinsically that life is not that way.

Simply put, we must consider other possibilities. Resist the urge to take the short path and assume you know all the data. Ask some additional questions to ascertain additional information and see if you shift your initial thought or perspective. It's the single most important thing I strive to achieve.

Lesson Twelve: Always Have Fun

For many years, when I would enter a room, one of my brothers-in-law would always say hi by calling me *Karon*! Which is just a funny way to say *Karen*. I always loved the way he said it, and all of us would usually laugh. It was his signature style.

A few months back, I was lamenting how Jennifer Lopez (J-Lo) could have a cool moniker but how K-Moon just wasn't working for me. Then I remembered my brother-in-law's voice, and the light bulb went off! K'Ron was born! After a whopping five dollars spent on fiverr.com, I now had a logo to use. My friend said to me, "Now, where exactly are you going to use that?" To which I replied, "Where am I *not* going to use it?"

Of course, this whole thing is silly, but it also serves a purpose. Our lives are busy, hectic, and stressful, and we often forget to slow down and just have fun. We watch kids play all the time but think for some reason that we don't need to as well. And some of us have forgotten how to do it! But it's the art of having fun and being silly from time to time that releases the stress that may be building. Engage your inner child and do something silly and fun. Even if it's only singing in the shower.

How Important Is It?

It goes without saying that our lives are more complicated, busy, and chaotic than ever. I hear from my clients about the frustration they feel for the never-ending list. "I need to exercise more but can't find the time," or "I need to spend time on myself, but there are always higher priorities." Years ago, I read in a running magazine to run first thing in the morning so that nothing during the day would get in the way of your exercise because you'd already done it! That really stuck with me, and to this day, I get up early each morning to exercise. It's important to me so I protect it.

What do you want to do but can't seem to get on the priority list? It may simply be a matter of time management, or it might be something deeper. Is time or money the real reason you have put something off, for example, going back to school? Or is there something underneath the desire that is holding you back? Somewhere, someone busier than you is exercising. Someone with less means than you is going back to school. So, what is the real reason you aren't taking the next step? Until you come to terms with the protector within you that has a fear of change, you can never truly move forward. Don't silence the voice inside; partner with it. Acknowledge the voice so you can understand the root concerns. Embodying the voice of the protector, journal this week—without judgment. Just let her be heard. You may be surprised at what she has to say.

Key Takeaways

- The most challenging parts of your life are creating your character and developing your voice.
- Being a leader takes preparation, continuous practice, and reflection.
- What element of transformation is important to you, and will you protect it?

My Takeaways

_____

_____

_____

_____

_____

_____

_____

_____

_____

_____

_____

_____

_____

_____

_____

_____

_____

_____

_____

_____

Action Steps

- What has been the pivotal decision so far in your life? What are the lessons you are taking away from it?
- Identify what inspires you and how you can keep it present in your life.
- Find your tribe. Keep trying out new groups until you find one that fits you.
- Write your obituary. How does it describe your impact?

My Action Items

_____

_____

_____

_____

_____

_____

_____

_____

_____

_____

_____

_____

_____

_____

_____

_____

_____

_____

_____

_____

Summary

S ooner or later in your career, something will happen to you or around you that will test you mentally. It will make you doubt yourself, question your actions, or make you feel isolated. And while that can be unsettling, having the foundation of your own positive self-beliefs will anchor you.

Understanding your values, talents, and really what it means to provide yourself with self-care is the basis for who are—the most unique "you." Some of us have spent a lifetime blending in or aligning to others, and we have lost our own unique voice. When we are able to find it (or recapture it), there is a balance that is returned to our lives. We are less inclined to continuously compare to others but rather evaluate our actions to our own internal guideposts. After all, as Theodore Roosevelt said, "Comparison is the thief of joy."

With your leadership feet now on stable ground, surround yourself with community. Find the board of directors, mentors, coaches, and sponsors who will help provide the supportive space for you to reach, stretch, and grow your leadership voice. Start a lean-in circle to grow other future leaders. As you make the inevitable mistakes, embrace them and grow from them. Share with others so they, too, can learn and see that being a leader does not also mean being perfect. Create your own list of leadership lessons so you can share them as you serve on someone else's board of directors.

To be the authentic leader you were meant to be, you must spend time being introspective. Always evaluate if who you are "being" is in alignment with who you truly are. This book is merely a starting point for you to dig deeper. I challenge you to join me on the lifelong journey to become a better leader in all aspects of our lives.

Afterword

True transformation does not occur quickly. I like to think of the analogy of a quilt. Quilts are made slowly, over time, and with focused work; once you've made progress, you would never dream of taking apart the squares.

Your leadership journey is the same. It takes time and adjustment as you navigate your life. Chances are you, too, will be thrown a curveball. While you may not appreciate it at the time, once you are past the storm, you will be able to look back and realize the lessons you can take from the experience. Use the event to help you lead others.

By nature, I am a lifelong learner. I thoroughly enjoy the journey of new knowledge; to that end, I have included a list of resources and my favorite things. I hope they keep you inspired to be the change that is in order.

My Favorite Things

Podcasts

Happier with Gretchen Rubin
This Is Your Life with Michael Hyatt
TED Radio Hour on NPR
Gallup Theme Thursday (covers StrengthsFinder talent themes)
The Way I Heard It with Mike Rowe
WTF with Marc Maron (adult language, not for everyone)
StoryCorps by NPR

Books

I Will Not Die an Unlived Life, Dawna Markova
Managing Brand You, Jerry Wilson and Ira Blumenthal
True North, Bill George
Now, Discover Your Strengths, Marcus Buckingham and Donald Clifton
Lean In, Sheryl Sandberg
The Soul Support Book, Deb Koffman

Facebook Pages

"Like" these pages, and they'll add inspiration and joy to your newsfeed:

A Mighty Girl
Hay House Daily Meditations
Trust Your Journey
You've Got This
The Road to ME
Dogs Are Family

Blogs

      KarenTransforms.com/blog.html
      ZenHabits.net by Leo Babauta

Websites

      ChopraCenterMeditation.com
      GallupStrenthsFinder.com
      CoachFederation.org

About the Author

Karen Mooney, MBA, ACC, is an <u>International Coaching Federation</u>–certified coach, a keynote speaker, and a blogger. She is a <u>Gallup StrengthsFinder</u>–certified instructor who leverages the assessment to help leaders transform their teams' talents into competitive advantages. For twenty years, she has led a facilities team at a large health-care organization in the Texas Medical Center, where she was awarded "Best Boss" (2010), and has been a two-time finalist for the institutional mentoring award. Karen's programs focus on women's leadership, women in the construction industry, and leading change in organizations.

Karen graduated from Texas A&M University with a degree in construction management and received her masters of business administration from the University of Texas at Tyler. She lives in a suburb of Houston, Texas, with Keith, her husband of more than twenty years, and their two dogs, Brady and Izzy. She's an avid runner—having completed over nine half marathons and one full marathon—and is a lover of all sports.

Karen can be followed at:

KarenTransforms.com
Facebook.com/KarenTransforms
Twitter.com/KarenTransforms

www.ingramcontent.com/pod-product-compliance
Lightning Source LLC
Chambersburg PA
CBHW060611200326
41521CB00007B/739

* 9 780692 820889 *